The old-time pamphlet ethos is back, with some of the most challenging work being done today. Prickly Paradigm Press is devoted to giving serious authors free rein to say what's right and what's wrong about their disciplines and about the world, including what's never been said before. The result is intellectuals unbound, writing unconstrained and creative texts about meaningful matters.

"Long live Prickly Paradigm Press.... Long may its flaming pamphlets lift us from our complacency."
—Ian Hacking

Prickly Paradigm is marketed and distributed by
The University of Chicago Press.

www.press.uchicago.edu

A list of current and future titles can be found ˌ
website and at the back of this pamphl

www.prickly-paradigm.c

Executive Publisher
Marshall Sahlins

Publishers
Peter Sahlins
Ramona Naddaff
Seminary Co-op Bookstore

Editor
Matthew Engelke
info@prickly-paradigm.com

Design and layout by Daniel Murphy.

Can a Liberal Be a Chief?
Can a Chief Be a Liberal?

Can a Liberal Be a Chief?
Can a Chief Be a Liberal?
Some Thoughts on an Unfinished Business of Colonialism

Olúfẹ́mi Táíwò

PRICKLY PARADIGM PRESS
CHICAGO

Prickly Paradigm Press, LLC
5629 South University Avenue
Chicago, IL 60637

www.prickly-paradigm.com

ISBN: 9781734643527
LCCN: 2021946572

Printed in the United States of America on acid-free paper.

I dedicate this book to the students in my Advanced Political Philosophy Seminar in the Rain Semester, 1988, at the Department of Philosophy, Obafemi Awolowo University, Ile-Ife, Nigeria. This originated as a prompt for one of their assignments. I can only hope they are not as stingy as their teacher in grading this!

Contents

Acknowledgements

As we say in Yorùbá, to fail to offer gratitude to one's benefactors is as bad as having robbed them of their gifts. I hope the day never dawns when I fail to express appreciation to those who continue to offer me gifts. And I cannot think of better gifts in our line of work than the work of friends, colleagues, students, and other associates, who are our interlocutors, who alert us to unclarities in our thinking, infelicities in our expression, track errors in our accounts and, just generally, save us from going to the public in our worst presentation.

Adejare Oladosu and Ebenezer Obadare went over and above what I have a right to expect in their work on this book. Each gave me written comments, quite extensive and detailed in Oladosu's case. They asked me questions that only those invested in my putting my best foot forward would have forced me to address. My student and research assistant, Zeyad El Nabolsy came late to this project, yet managed to influence the final shape with his comments and suggestions. John Ayotunde Isola Bewaji read the work and was unsparing in his reaction to the work. I am profoundly grateful for their help.

The reviewer for the press deserves my gratitude for reading the manuscript with tremendous care and sensitivity, raising concerns my responses to which have vastly improved the final product and recommending publication despite concerns that might have made others do the opposite.

Earlier versions of the work have benefited from the reactions of those present at sessions at the 25th Annual Conference of the International Society for African Philosophy and Studies held at Mississippi State University, Starkville, Mississippi and the Caribbean Philosophical Association Annual Conference on "Shifting the Geography of Reason XVI: Resistance, Reparation, Renewal", held at Brown University, Providence, Rhode Island, both in 2019. I thank the participants for their interventions that have contributed to this work.

Finally, I could not have asked for a better editor than Matthew Engelke whose work on this book from my first contact with him has been helpful and productive of insights that have significantly improved it.

I thank you all.

Olúfẹ́mi Táíwò
Ithaca, New York
January 2021.

Introduction

Can a liberal be a chief? Can a chief be a liberal? These are my questions. Yet readers need to know how I am approaching them, especially against the background of "African Studies."

The literature on chieftaincy in Africa is dominated by history and anthropology, with political science coming not too far behind. Yet, in the present work, I have elected not to engage directly with these dominant discourses. Certainly, one could always perform the dodge of claiming a lack of familiarity with or competence in the respective disciplines. But one can always get up to speed in the respective discourses and deploy insights from them in one's preferred sphere while arguing, as best one can, with whatever one derives from them. That approach does not avail in my case.

My interest in chieftaincy is deeper and more catholic in its scope than what often motivates empirical studies: discrete explorations—description, analyses, explanation—of specific communities and the operations of chieftaincies in them. Efforts are often made to account for their historical evolution, the specific culture-bound values that legitimate them and in virtue of which they command the assent of those who subscribe to them and abide by their dictates, their relations to other institutions within the same society or in comparative perspectives, and similar concerns. Of course, I must not omit to point out that, where Africa is concerned, there is the usual unhelpful, even if widespread, insistence on dubious generalizations when it comes to the operations of chieftaincy in diverse African contexts.

This work aims to move the discussion to a different sphere, one that is, I think, more germane to how the institutions and practices pertaining to chieftaincy have evolved and why a failure to take seriously the philosophical foundations of such institutions and practices may explain the severe crises that characterize them in the present. In other words, I am concerned with the very concept of chieftaincy and how it has evolved historically as a form of rule that has certain features that transcend cultural spheres; every instance of chieftaincy is an empirical exemplar of this general kind. This approach allows for a more dynamic apprehension of the relevant phenomena. I treat both the core concepts in the work—chieftaincy and liberalism—as "universals" and seek to unravel how their interactions in the African continent represent contingent iterations that allow us to compare them to similar examples in other parts of the world. The argument is supported by illustrations from current events and historical phenomena but does not rely on them for its validity. Indeed, I want to start with some examples, as they allow us to appreciate both the complexity of the situation on the ground and the purchase of my approach. Can a chief be a liberal? Can a liberal be a chief? No, and no.

I do not deny that advances have been made by history, anthropology, and political science in the discourse on chieftaincy in Africa. I am more interested in the philosophical issues raised by the phenomenon, particularly when it comes to the relationship between chieftaincy and liberalism in light of ongoing developments in the continent.

Framing the Problem

On March 23, 2015, Goodwill Zwelithini, a South African citizen, in a conversation with some fellow citizens, expressed his opinion that, when it came to immigration to South Africa, it was way past time to shut the door and, what is more, ask foreigners in the country to pack up and leave. Around the same time, April 2015, in Nigeria, Rilwan Akiolu, a Nigerian citizen, domiciled in Lagos, in conversation with a group of fellow citizens resident in the same city but of a different nationality within the country, declared that if the community made up of his interlocutors did not support his candidate in the upcoming gubernatorial elections in Lagos State, he would cause the spirit of the ocean—Lagos is a port city—to visit death and destruction on them. South Africa and Nigeria are no different from other countries in the world. And the prejudices expressed by our respective speakers are not rare in our world. We have witnessed similar sentiments in recent years from Donald Trump, Viktor Orbán, and many others.

To that extent, the sentiments may have been vile but the right of citizens to express their opinions is irreproachable. This is routine in any society, except those under despotic rule in modern times. However, Zwelithini's utterances were blamed for triggering a wave of murderous xenophobic attacks on immigrants in South Africa, and many countries had to scramble to arrange the repatriation of their citizens from there. And, in Nigeria, Mr. Akiolu was accused of hinting at ethnic cleansing and propagating hate speech directed specifically at the ethnic group whence came his inter-locutors in the meeting to which I alluded above. And Donald Trump has been repeatedly excoriated for his slurs against certain categories of immigrants. Why is this so? It is not every time a citizen says vile things that riots result, even if the citizen concerned is an important one. Nor do we routinely entertain fears of outbreaks of violent conflict on account of someone saying some-thing. Certainly, the attack on the Capitol in the United States on January 6, 2021, is the most recent reminder that words do have consequences. Still, while such events do occur, they are rare. Nevertheless, we need to explain why things *threatened to*, in Nigeria, and *did*, in South Africa, go haywire.

To be sure, neither Mr. Zwelithini nor Mr. Akiolu is a "citizen" in the ordinary sense of that word, either in the English language or in their respective domains. Domains? Yes. Both are royals; more specif-ically, they are kings, no less. Goodwill Zwelithini was the King of Zululand; Rilwan Akiolu is the King of Lagos, a Yorùbá city that doubles as Nigeria's commercial and cultural capital. In other words, they are both potentates of the indigenous modes of governance, "the chieftaincy,"[1] as one scholar dubs it, whose legitimacy derives primarily from a complex of rules, practices, and processes that are, in significant respects, autochthonous.

Although I hesitate to adopt this terminology, deployed with care and nuance (as I hope to do), it serves well the purposes of this discussion. It might be easier to adopt "monarchical rule" for this discussion. After all, the two figures referred to above, Mr. Zwelithini and Mr. Akiolu, are monarchs. But chieftaincy is a more expansive category than monarchy and, as we shall see presently, the insistence by colonizers that African potentates could not enjoy the same status as those who had subdued them and, therefore, could not continue to be addressed or treated as monarchs, is responsible for what we deal with now. It is responsible for the false identification, in the literature on chieftaincy, of the mode as a peculiar feature of the colonies or, in the context of colonialism-inflected anthropology, other backward societies (whereas, for metropolitan formations, there were no chiefs but monarchs). This mischaracterization explains in part why others have not happened upon the path taken in this discussion. Given that part of what I argue here is that the problem of chieftaincy and liberalism is present where we have a coexistence of the two phenomena, it helps to deploy a term that allows us to think more globally than within the contexts of single communities. Additionally, not all communities in which chieftaincies are discernible as such rise to the level of monarchies, and our scope is meant to be as capacious as possible.

Certainly, were we to restrict ourselves to a discussion of the mode of governance of a single community—the Ashanti Empire or the Ọ̀yọ́ Empire, say—we would have to adopt the method deployed by J. E. Casely Hayford in his book designed to convince the British colonizers that the peoples of the Gold Coast, now Ghana, were not primitives with backward, simple institutions but, on the contrary, sophisticated peoples who had evolved superior institutions, especially in the area of governance. His was an attempt at capturing the complexities of these institutions.

> The term "chief" is in the present day used indiscriminately to represent a king, a chief, or even a headman of a village. It is a careless use of the word. The foreigner, unable or lacking the patience to discern between one native authority and another, groups them all under the designation "chief." Let me try to bring order out of chaos.[2]

One would wish that contemporary scholars paid attention to scholarship from some of our pioneer modern thinkers, before we begin to repeat what he clearly deemed "careless use." But since my concern here is with the general idea of governance by chieftaincy, and not with elucidating the relationship between monarchs and chiefs but between rulers and ruled, I hope that I am not guilty of "careless use."

The imposition of formal colonialism led to the imbrication of these local modes of governance within a qualitatively different complex of rules, practices, and processes. The problem is that the colonial authorities incorporated the chieftaincy into the colonial system and, in so doing, managed profoundly to change the institution and its appurtenant practices and processes, in ways that are not always clear or helpful. Colonial rule undermined in some cases, altered in others, and distorted in yet others, the constitutive principles as well as legitimating grounds of the chieftaincy before colonialism. One thing is certain: chieftaincies in Africa were nothing like they were in any part of the continent once they were touched by colonialism. Worse, in certain areas where there was no chieftaincy, or at least no significant exemplar of the phenomenon, colonialism forced some on them.[3] These developments would have serious repercussions on the presentation of the problem addressed in this essay.

Can a liberal be a chief? Can a chief be a liberal? As I have said: no, on both counts. The reason is very simple. However we expatiate on the idea of chieftaincy, it is almost impossible to accommodate it within the framework of the political philosophy of liberalism and the representative democracy it legitimizes as the preferred mode of governance in the modern age. The metaphysical underpinnings of a liberal regime require that the subject to be governed be sovereign and bound by the dictates of that rule to which she has given her consent. But to be able to give her consent, she must be free and equal, even if only putatively, with all others in association with whom she is instituting a governance scheme, and those put in charge of running this scheme must themselves be subordinate to its authority.

No doubt, conceptually, we may be able to formulate a chieftaincy that meets the criteria we just outlined. However, historically, in terms of both institutional forms and ideas about such forms, even when we are able to point to instances of chieftaincies with some elective elements in them, I do not think it is an exaggeration to say that the elements we have identified with liberalism as a political philosophy and its associated political regimes are exclusive to the modern age in the annals of the history of political philosophy and practice.

The literature on the role of chieftaincy in African politics and administration hardly ever addresses the questions I pose. Furthermore, I do not know of any other exploration of the issue from the perspective of political philosophy. In undertaking such an exploration, we do not place chieftaincy outside political philosophy. We argue, instead, that African chieftaincies, like their counterparts elsewhere in the world, were at different times products of philosophical efforts by their home societies to answer one of the central questions of political philosophy: Who ought to rule when not all can rule? This is what enables us to compare chiefly and liberal regimes in terms of their respective legitimating philosophical principles. This is what sets our discussion apart.

Prior to the imposition of modern-inflected, European colonialism, African polities were marked by a medley of modes of governance as well as a diverse array of political formations. Not all had chieftaincies in them; there were small communities that barely rose to the level of states and, to that extent, had few or no ruling institutions or rulers. Those with chieftaincies, too, were a motley of state forms: some were multistate confederacies; others were monoethnic royal kingdoms; still others were multination states marked by ethnic plurality and varieties of heterogeneity—linguistic, religious, political, and so on. Many were absolute monarchies; others involved monarchical rule established by aristocracy that pretty much circumscribed the boundaries of legitimacy in the relevant polity.[4] In this, Africa was no different from other continents through history.

From all indications, European colonialism's interventions in the modes of governance it found in its African colonies were guided by one supreme principle: secure the territories at the lowest cost possible to the colonizing power.[5] Keeping the colonized in check, pacifying the colonies, and just generally ensuring that the business of rapine—Africa was the land par excellence of exploitation-colonialism—that defined the dominant form that colonialism took in Africa remained on course. Yes, the colonialists proclaimed an additional aim for their forcing themselves on the colonized. No, they never denied the rapine; they only ever tried to sugarcoat it, by saying that, in the name of a dubious "dual mandate," they were also there to "civilize" their African subjects.[6] This is the idea that part of the reason for colonizing Africans was to bring them to modernity and remake Africans, their institutions, practices, and processes in the modern mode. But this was a lie, and nowhere is this lie better laid out than in colonial policies regarding what mode of governance Africans should have. Again, this lie continues to elude scholars of chieftaincy. We will see why below.

Colonialism did not intend to install, beyond a superficial level, the legitimating instruments of the system in the name of which it had in part justified its colonization of subject peoples: modernity and its sociopolitical inflection, liberal representative democracy. Hence was created the unfinished business of resolving the conflicts, inconsistencies, and contradictions between the old indigenous—including some autochthonous[7]—modes of governance dominated by chieftaincy, and the alien mode of governance founded on the consent of the governed and the equality of all. This is where it is crucial to state, in a way that is not often to be found in the discussion of chieftaincy and modern modes of governance, what sets modern modes of governance apart from other modes of governance that are nonmodern or premodern. We dispense with the usual epithets: "traditional" and "precolonial." There is a reason why the use of "precolonial" to describe African governance is problematic, and possibly obscure. It is a temporal horizon with no boundaries: it could refer to any period from the beginning of time to when colonial rule was introduced in any particular place in Africa. As a framework for periodization, it is completely useless. And, over time, almost every practice can become traditional; all it requires is to have the practice etched in the collective memory of a society and justified by appeal to its immemorial usage in the relevant society.

Historically, the dominant mode of governance in the modern age is governance by consent, based on the equality of all, governors and governed alike, even when chieftaincy is nominally present in it, and this is without regard to location or culture. Once we take seriously the global distribution of chieftaincy, especially during the period when colonialism was being clamped on the continent, it is easy to see how wrong it is to speak of it as if it were a primarily African phenomenon.

It is only when we embrace what I call "the metaphysics of difference," under which African phenomena are always construed in their difference from similar ones across the world, that this designation makes sense. Insofar as chieftaincy is an instance of monarchical, oligarchic, or aristocratic rule, marked by the rule of one, the few, or a small privileged class, the problem that it poses for liberalism is almost intrinsic, whether it occurs in Lagos or in Amsterdam, Kuala Lumpur, Seoul, or Bangkok. Whatever we say about the relationship between chieftaincy and liberalism must be applicable to all instances of its kind. The reason is simple. Whatever shades of difference there are between chieftaincies, unless they be established in a way other than by heredity or selection, the issue of their compatibility with liberalism and the mode of governance it recommends or legitimates would be salient. This is even more so given that, closer to its origins and up till our own time, liberalism has always made room for chiefly status within its operation. As will be shown presently, some who wish to justify their preference for the incorporation of chieftaincy into current liberal regimes cite this in support of their position. We shall be arguing against this possibility. The fact that liberalism can accommodate chieftaincy is why we may not assert any facile definitions of either concept or preselect preferred characterizations respecting them.

Africa and Europe: Parallels

To situate properly our contention that the question of chieftaincy and liberalism is not differently presented in Africa from how it is anywhere else in the world, let us explore some parallels with Europe. In the nineteenth century, the countries that became Africa's colonizers had themselves not become modern polities and some of them had not even become the nation-states they now are. What is more, their modes of governance had not become certifiably modern, and chieftaincy was no less salient in them. It is important to point this out because, in the discourse on chieftaincy and Africa, chieftaincy is treated as if the colonizing countries themselves were not dominated by chieftaincy. There is a simple explanation: while empire lasted, Britain could not recognize more than one reigning monarch in the realm. As a result of this exigency, all other monarchs in the empire, from Gambia to Malaysia, were reduced to "chiefs." The fact is that many of the local monarchs that had been subjugated by the colonizers had their own chiefs who were subordinate to them; such monarchs never saw themselves as anything but the supreme authorities in their respective realms, whatever their British colonial overlords thought, a point made by Casely Hayford, as we remarked above. That no effort was made by the colonizers to diminish the role or status of these "rulers"—who only had to acknowledge British suzerainty to keep their offices—is partly responsible for the problem that we tackle in this work. While that arrangement may have worked for colonizers to demarcate the lines of authority while colonialism lasted, it is unacceptable for scholars to maintain this expediency and ignore the identity of the phenomena they are studying. This is even more so once, as we make clear presently, some African monarchs before their realms were subjugated regarded themselves, and were so regarded by European monarchs, as the equals of other monarchs.[8] We must expand the boundaries of our concepts if indeed we are to come up with more plausible and more complete explanatory models.

When Lagos was seized by the British in 1861, it would be a stretch to say that liberal representative democracy had been the dominant mode of governance in the United Kingdom. There was still no universal franchise then, the House of Lords could override the House of Commons, even though the latter's members were popularly elected by qualified voters, excluding women and the poor, and the prime ministership was still the exclusive preserve of aristocrats. The country was pretty much dominated by chieftaincy. Additionally, debates were ongoing, evidenced by periodic reform bills designed to reduce, over time, the salience of chieftaincy and enhance the primacy of the popular will in the operations of the British political system. In other words, Britain was struggling to determine what to do with chieftaincy in its emergent liberal-democratic regime. Such was the salience of chieftaincy in British thought concerning governance that the archimperialists Frederick D. Lugard and Charles Temple used the commonalities between the British political hierarchy and that of the Sokoto Caliphate in Nigeria—each had a clearly delineated monarch, king and caliph, in charge in their respective spheres—to preselect the Fulani as the native group most suited to rule themselves and, in what Moses E. Ochonu has termed "colonialism by proxy," others (for example, the peoples of the country's Middle Belt region).[9] In 1861, Italy became a unified country under the Savoy chieftaincy. Germany was ten years away from unification under yet another chieftaincy, in this case Prussian. The fact that motley polities in Africa were under the sway of chieftaincies was nothing peculiar. This means that the problem of the relation between chieftaincy and liberal-representative democracy in Africa is just another iteration of a global problem the solution to which perforce would be benefited by a comparative understanding.

As I have argued elsewhere, in the nineteenth century, Africa, from the north to the south, was a veritable workshop of constitutional experiments concerned with making and remaking various polities.[10] It is curious that the discourse on chieftaincy in Africa hardly ever reckons with this history. The Sokoto Caliphate had been constituted at the turn of that century. Napoleon Bonaparte had inaugurated, if not a transition to modernity, at least a debate about the compatibility of modernity and Islam in Egypt with his invasion of the country, in 1798. The Ashanti Empire was at its apogee even as the Ọ̀yọ́ Empire was experiencing severe pressures occasioned by the spread northward of the ravages of the European slave trade. The Kingdom of Benin was stable in its political under-standing and practices. All these polities were under the sway of diverse chieftaincies characterized by differing degrees of coherence in the legitimating principles for their governance.

The upshot of all this is the falsity of opposing so-called traditional societies and their accompanying political institutions in Africa to equally so-called modern or, even more dubiously, Western equivalent ones. In fact, although liberalism was the fundamental political orientation under modernity in Europe, Europeans, both political theorists and practitioners, were still struggling with how to universalize the franchise while preserving rule by the bourgeoisie, whose dominance had marked the overthrow of the old regime at the inauguration of political modernity. Outside of Switzerland, there was nowhere in Europe where we can say that the problem was resolved in any definitive way that saw the final removal of chieftaincy from their political system till well into the twentieth century, with Greece being the most recent, in 1975; incidentally, this same year, Spain elected to reinstall chieftaincy at the apex of its state.

So, to talk of the Sokoto Caliphate, which was barely a hundred years old when the British subdued it, in 1903, as a "traditional society," and not the

Netherlands or even the United Kingdom, is mistaken and, I dare say, a mischaracterization. In fact, the Sokoto Caliphate was new, whereas the Ashanti Empire and the Kingdom of Benin were old. The Sokoto Caliphate was, in the annals of world history and the evolution of modes of governance in it, a novel form of rule, although one with antecedents in Egypt, Ottoman Turkey, and older forms of imamate\caliphate rule in the history of Islamic political thought. To put them all in the same category does not aid illumination of the problem to be solved.

Once we use governance by consent and the formal equality of all as the principal difference between modern and nonmodern modes of governance, we attain some clarity on how we might make sense of chieftaincy and the problem it poses for our efforts to install liberal regimes in polities marked by all the elements we associate with modern governance. To the extent that chieftaincy dominated African polities at the inception of colonialism, even if some African thinkers and leaders were already striving to remake their polities in the modern image—the Fanti Confederation is the best example—and even if we have chieftaincies where they incorporated some elective element—some Ghanaian kingdoms and city-states did have them—we may not say that those polities were either liberal or modern. That is, even if we say that the voice of the people is the voice of God, and that popular acceptance of (or at least acquiescence in) chieftaincy by the ruled in earlier societies was an indication of consent by the governed, that would not make them instances of modern liberal regimes.

This differentia is often obscured, both by African thinkers who wish to argue that African societies of old were already democratic and therefore need not learn democracy from anywhere else[11] and by Euro-American ideologues who wish to argue that the West has always been modern or that all of the West is modern. Neither the Ashanti Empire nor the Kingdom of Italy at roughly equivalent periods of the nineteenth century could be said to have embodied the principle of governance by consent, even though each had selection principles that often involved participation by classes beyond the hereditary rulers and their associated aristocracies. In fact, Ashanti chieftaincy had more elective content than the Italian dynasties at the time. And it would be a stretch to say that Portugal and Spain before 1974 and 1975, respectively, were any more modern in governance terms than Kwame Nkrumah's Ghana or Julius Nyerere's Tanzania. Indeed, one could make a case that Botswana was a liberal regime at a time when Spaniards were under the jackboots of Francisco Franco's fascist enforcers.

Chieftaincy as a Philosophical Problem: Who Ought to Rule?

The approach taken in this work is distinctive. It places the question of chieftaincy directly in the discourse of political philosophy, makes no room for its "Africanness," historicizes the idea in ways that are rarely found in the literature and, ultimately, locates it in the present, a present that is marked all across the continent by ongoing attempts to install liberal-representative democracies in our various countries.

Because of my conviction that, however sophisticated, a strictly conceptual analysis of chieftaincy and liberalism is bound to fall short in most situations, and because concepts have histories that affect their embodiment in real institutions, practices, and processes, this analysis is designed to show two things. First, chieftaincy has evolved over time in various societies, as a human contraption, and to that extent we may not treat it as if it were peculiar to Africa, or as if its "Africanness"—whatever that means—conferred an iota of illumination on our analysis of it. Certainly, if, as we argue, the iteration of chieftaincy and liberalism has a specific historical framework in which it is presented, it makes sense to lay out that evolution in some detail. Second, we limit our scope to the career of chieftaincy in the philosophical discourse of modernity in which liberalism is the dominant, if not the go-to, political philosophy. It is only in the context provided by the effort to install liberal democracy or some variant of it that the problem of chieftaincy that interests us has any resonance. If, for some reason, African countries were to elect to restore various indigenous forms of rule overturned by colonialism and give up entirely on installing regimes of rule inspired by liberal-representative democracy, our whole discussion would lack a raison d'être!

When we look at the available philosophical treatments of chieftaincy in the literature, all the preceding steps are not present. Whether for or against chieftaincy, such treatments usually assume that there is chieftaincy and there is democracy. In this context, the defenders of chieftaincy are not interested in it as a historical phenomenon. And when they indicate an awareness of the historicity of the phenomenon, they barely trace out the implications of the changes they identify for the core problems of legitimacy that occupy us here. On the contrary, these defenders treat chieftaincy almost as if it were an essential part of African governance, and as if what were called for was to defend it against unwarranted charges that it is incompatible with democracy. But hardly is there any effort to consider democracy, too, as a historical and variegated phenomenon, and when the issue is raised, it is to reaffirm the democraticness of African governance within the context of pushing back against racism or foreign criticism.

I start from the assumption that chieftaincy is an attempt by the people who institute it to answer one of political philosophy's central questions: Who may rule, given that not all can rule? Answers to this question provide justification and legitimacy for political arrangements under which some exercise power and others are required to obey, and they range from divine ordainment to social contract. Whether monarchical, oligarchic, or aristocratic, chieftaincy is not known, historically, as being based on popular consent; conversely, we know that democracy, whether direct or indirect in its representative dimension, is always associated with popular rule and is regarded as distorted, if not abandoned, when it is established in any of the forms of chieftaincy. As we indicate presently, when either form of governance is not considered in this historical and conceptual framework, but instead conceived of in terms of cultural identity or contingent societal realizations, much confusion is generated.

Whether it is designed by individuals or emerges over time from social relations within a given society, chieftaincy must be understood as that society's pragmatic answer to the challenge of determining the criteria for assigning, to one or a few, the power to direct, control, and govern others, while providing those others with grounds for obeying their rulers. The question of who may rule is indissolubly linked to the question of legitimacy and obligation to obey the dictates of the rulers.

Posing the question this way reinserts discourse about African phenomena into the discourse of the perennial question of legitimate rule and political obligation and its realization in our time in the context of chieftaincy and liberalism. It enables us to question assumptions undergirding the easy characterizations of African governance systems as democratic, based on consent, and elective, with zero attention paid to issues of identity and anti-racism.

Let us now examine some of the extant philosophical treatments in the literature. We should resist the temptation to dismiss all previous forms of rule marked by chieftaincy as incorrigible despotisms. There should be no doubt that in many old, advanced societies they all took seriously Jean-Jacques Rousseau's quip that for rule to survive and prosper, rulers must transmute might into right. "The strongest is never strong enough to be always the master unless he transforms might into right and obedience into duty."[12] Though fear may compel obedience, some form of acceptance, not mere acquiescence, must have undergirded rule before the modern epoch. That is, consent of the governed is not a newfangled principle of rule in human society procured by modernity. But the character of consent in the two cases does differ. And the grounds of legitimacy are dissimilar, too. More about this anon.

Unfortunately, while the anti-colonial struggle lasted and since formal independence was won, African intellectuals have scarcely engaged with the philosophical problem posed by this unfinished business. The discussion has been dominated by anthropologists, historians, and political scientists who are, in turn, preoccupied by empirical methodologies and pragmatic questions respecting what political system works best. For the most part, the debate is dominated by what I would call identitarian frameworks, advanced by both scholars and practitioners, in which attention is riveted on chieftaincy as if it were a defining element in African identity, personal and group, and its absence would represent an irremediable loss. Treatment from the philosophical neck of the woods has been minimal: that is, philosophers have not addressed chieftaincy in particular societies as an answer, at different times, to one of the central questions of political philosophy: Who ought to rule when not all can rule? What are the bases of political legitimacy for having some rule and others obey?

Political philosophy should be taken seriously, and African modes of governance should be treated similarly to their equivalents in other areas of the world. There may be more philosophical treatments out there than I am aware of or have access to. Be that as it may, I am convinced that the philosophical problem posed by chieftaincy to liberalism deserves serious attention, and that this attention is warranted by ongoing attempts in the continent to install liberal-democratic regimes in contexts where chieftaincies remain a salient presence.

Let us consider some notable exceptions. I start with contemporary thinkers. I argue that contemporary philosophers' lack of historical awareness vitiates their description of the problem and that their willingness to treat it as one of cultural identity rather than the philosophical issue of legitimacy and obligation—who deserves to rule when not all can rule, or what is the best constitution—limits their insights.

In "Monarchy and Democracy: Towards a Cultural Renaissance," Joe Teffo, as befits a philosopher, posed the question of liberalism and chieftaincy at the level of choosing what political system is best for a given society; in this case, that of South Africa in the postapartheid dispensation. He contends that South Africa, in light of the checkered history of politics and political systems in postindependence Africa,

> stands a unique chance to break new ground in the creation of a better system of democracy informed by her history, the present political conditions, and what has obtained, and still obtains in the name of democracy in post-independence or post-colonial Africa.[13]

To this end, Teffo would like South Africa to abandon the idea that monarchy and democracy are incompatible. His reasons are many, from the fact that "traditional leaders," chiefs, in comparison to elected officials, are closer to and enjoy more political legitimacy with rural dwellers, to the persistence of monarchy in other democracies (*MD*, 5).

> Thus, I submit that kingship and chieftaincy are, not to the exclusion of elections, traditional bases for political legitimacy. They confer legitimate power. It is absurd that in South Africa the constitution is purporting to do the same. We dare not underestimate the importance of rural people and rural political culture for stability and the healthy development of our society (*MD*, 6).

It turns out that, for Teffo, constitutional democracy inspired by what he called, following Ali

Mazrui, the Western piece of South Africa's "triple heritage," cannot but be incomplete if it is not in harmony with the "indigenous" piece of that heritage. "A balance will therefore have to be found between the need for democratically elected rural local authorities and the constitutional provisions guaranteeing the existence of the institution of traditional authorities" (*MD*, 7). Teffo canvassed a constitutional role for "traditional leaders," who "are crucial to any constitutional dispensation because they remain in touch with the majority of the people who reside in the rural areas" (*MD*, 6).

> To this end, I will argue that the adoption of traditional institutions, which were neglected in favour of wholesale classical democracy and other alien ideologies, will go a long way in assisting us in fashioning a dispensation unique to our situation. My plea is for an Afrocentric cultural renaissance. South Africa is a young nation with an identity crisis, trying its best to stand on its feet. Thus critical inputs by citizens and a responsive government could only assist South Africa to grow a better understanding of itself as a nation state. South Africa is unique in that here the African and Western streams meet and can flow together harmoniously. Despite this harmony, the Afro-centric cultural dimension is calling for more respect and space to express itself positively. A contextual democracy responding to South African actuality ought to be developed (*MD*, 1).

Teffo's core claim is that monarchy and other "traditional" modes of governance in South Africa ought to be integrated into the constitutional framework of the country's governance. Apart from the alleged incompleteness of a system that ignores local histories and practices, there is a pragmatic insistence that not including those indigenous institutions and their associated processes and practices explains the many inadequacies of governance and people's alienation from it in relevant jurisdictions. Finally, Teffo argues vigorously that the premium placed on elections, as important as they are, is liable to obscure the specific role of chieftaincy in the constitution of African societies, and this role is no less present in other countries outside the continent, such as the United Kingdom or the Netherlands. Just as those European democracies can accommodate chieftaincy in them, African monarchies are no less compatible with democracy, given the role that consensus plays within them.[14] The presence of a chieftaincy in a liberal-democratic regime does not mean that the institution is an integral part of the democratic system. Often, chieftaincy is preserved without salience, is made subservient to popular control, often serves a totemic purpose as an embodiment of the state and a unifier of everybody in the polity, which is like Teffo's own submission regarding accommodating chieftaincy in the constitutional order. But it is not clear to me that Teffo is thinking of mere ceremonial presence for monarchies within his preferred governance model.

Teffo's work deserves attention because his is a defense of the relevance, if not the necessity, of chieftaincy in contemporary Africa. He went beyond the usual pedigree and identitarian arguments that I alluded to above. Yet, I would like to argue that its pragmatic and identitarian thrust did not allow the discussion to take seriously the issues that we canvass here. Let us assume that, as Teffo and many other commentators contend, we can reduce the alienation the governed feel from their government in the rural areas still dominated by chieftaincy; I do not think that that is enough or that alienation from government and inefficient administration are the most significant ills that the issue of chieftaincy and liberalism engenders. We shall come back to this presently.[15]

J. Michael Williams offers a sophisticated and detailed analysis of the legitimacy of chieftaincy in a state that is structured by a liberal-democratic regime. The core issue in *Chieftaincy, the State, and Democracy* "is how the chieftaincy seeks to establish and maintain its political legitimacy, vis-à-vis local populations as well as the state, in the post-apartheid period."[16] Williams, too, is very clear that the question of the legitimacy of chieftaincy is engendered by the new reality in postapartheid South Africa, where,

> since 1994, the chieftaincy has been forced to share its authority with a new set of institutions, which are based on a set of norms, rules, and processes that are distinct from its own. For example, one obvious difference is that while post-apartheid institutions are premised on the twin principles of majority rule and free and fair elections, the chieftaincy is based on decision making through consensus and on the hereditary right to rule. Similarly, while the ANC [African National Congress] promotes the vision of a pluralist and diverse South Africa, many people in rural areas perceive the chieftaincy as representative of the unity of the local community, and in many cases "strangers" are met with distrust. (*CSD*, 2–3)

Williams's framing of the problem he set out to illuminate captures quite succinctly the outline of our own concern. We know that "the principles of majority rule and free and fair elections" are usually regarded as emblematic of liberal-democratic regimes, and liberal-representative democracy is what postapartheid South Africa is striving to install as its preferred state type. The rest of the passage articulates the peculiar problem that the accommodation of chieftaincy within the framework of a liberal-democratic state characterized by pluralism—nationalities, ethnicities, interests, cultures, and so on—poses, not, in our case, for the legitimacy of chieftaincy but for its relevance and for the appropriateness of its deployment in a new political form where its legitimating underpinnings do not encompass all who now inhabit its putative jurisdiction.

Williams's discussion contains significant insights into the problem of chieftaincy and liberalism. During the debate over the South African constitution, for instance, "After the [1994] election ... there was pressure from women's organizations, progressive ANC members, and other civil society organizations to limit the authority of the chieftaincy in the final constitution" (*CSD*, 86). Chiefs, for their part, "wanted 'customary law' to trump other constitutional provisions, such as the equality clause" (*CSD*, 88). Ultimately,

> the CC [Constitutional Court] made it clear that traditional leaders would have to learn to fit within a democratic order, not the other way around. ... Even though the 1996 constitution protects the institution to some degree, there is an underlying belief

(at least among those in the CC) that the role of the chieftaincy will be limited by the 1996 constitution (*CSD*, 89).

What Williams's discussion brings into clear relief is that the critical issue may not be one of whether chieftaincy can be integrated into a liberal constitutional order. Teffo got it right: this is routinely done in other liberal democracies like the United Kingdom and Norway. Rather, the critical issue is more likely to be one of what the implications are for the operation of the respective regimes when it comes to the rights, entitlements, and forbearances that are the meat and potatoes of a liberal order. This is the issue that contentions like Teffo's elide. Teffo is not alone. This issue is not routinely addressed in much of the philosophical literature on chieftaincy in Africa. The critical questions are not whether chieftaincy is important at the local level or can enhance the effectiveness of government or the efficient delivery of government services or even enhance the legitimacy of the state.[17] As important as those questions are, even more important are whether chieftaincy should be retained and how we address the many conundrums it generates respecting both the constitutive principles of a liberal regime and chieftaincy's implications for the rights of the individual in such a polity.

This is a good place to introduce the only case known to me of an African philosopher who calls for the abolition—yes, abolition—of "the institution of traditional kingship." Adejare Oladosu is impatient with a "fundamental failing" in how Africa organizes life and thought at the present time: that is, "Africa's seeming inability to govern itself well."[18] This, he contends, is, at bottom, "a failure of philosophy, specifically, a failure of constitutional philosophy" (*DVRC*, 46). The solution he proffers is "the adoption of a full-fledged republican constitutional order by contemporary African states" (*DVRC*, 46). Against the widespread preference for what he terms "some form of a mixed constitution," for example, as we saw above in Teffo and Williams in the case of South Africa, Oladosu argues

> for the adoption of an unmitigated form of republicanism. I assume that modern Africans, like people everywhere, desire—or at least ought to desire—democratic governance. ... My defence of republicanism is informed by a fundamental conviction, namely, that only a full-fledged republican order can provide the constitutional anchor for a true democracy (*DVRC*, 47).

As indicated in the introduction, I share Oladosu's radical preference. I think, though, that his argument could use more nuance when it comes to his recommendation of republicanism. Neither republicanism nor liberalism comes in only one hue. Liberalism cannot feature chieftaincy as an integral element—the latter never can accommodate the equality of all—but republicanism did not start with popular sovereignty.[19] And the insistence that "democracy can only thrive in a republic" (*DVRC*, 48) is undermined by the history of republics that were not necessarily democratic—the United States would be a prime example for much of its history.

Oladosu argues that the case against traditional kingship in Africa—he seems to think that kingships in other climes may at least have some claim to legitimacy—rests on the absence of "justice at its foundation":

> It is my contention that the institution of traditional kingship in Africa was founded either on the coercive imperatives of might and naked force, being the prize of war and conquest, or on what we may describe as spiritual deception, the practical manifestation of a dubious theology (*DVRC*, 49).

He cites the examples of the constitution of the Sokoto Caliphate and the incorporation of the Ibadan state, both in what is now called Nigeria, in the nineteenth century, as evidence of the founding of two monarchies on conquest and violence. And the entire institution of traditional kingship in Yorùbá country is established on a mythological basis deriving from the eponymous founder Odùduwà and the legitimacy to rule of Yorùbá ọba originating from their descendance from Odùduwà. He concludes that neither violence nor myth suffices to ground legitimacy when it comes to the question of who ought to rule when not all can rule. As if this were not bad enough, he charges the institution in its African iteration with being bereft of any "social utility (in the course of African history)" or "contemporary relevance" (*DVRC*, 52).

Oladosu may have overstated his case against the legitimacy of "traditional kingship." To his contention that only might was the basis of the legitimacy of African kingship: unless he is working with an abbreviated history of the institution across Africa, he should have accounted for the longevity of the institution, for its stability, and for its acceptance, at some level (and not mere acquiescence in it), by vast populations that have lived under it till the present.[20] In a rejoinder to this criticism of his article, Oladosu has insisted that nothing short of acceptance is acceptable to him as the ground of legitimacy and that, in the political sphere, this can only be expressed through consent:

> So, if consent means acceptance, and I should contend that that is the only meaningful sense of consent in this context, then I would find it difficult to impute it to Africans who lived or are currently living under monarchies (personal communication).

I insist that the history of political philosophy, especially liberalism, does not support this position. Rousseau got it right: might must become right to immunize itself against repeated challenges.

The whole problem of political obligation in political philosophy is centered precisely on the recognition of the insufficiency of might and the necessity of founding obligation on normative grounds. I believe that it is not enough to express dissatisfaction with the operation of African "traditional kingship." We should not represent it as a simple, unsophisticated institution. The evidence indicates otherwise, although I do not go into that here.[21]

The rest of Oladosu's discussion in the article turns on critical responses to African philosophers who have argued for the continuing relevance of monarchies in Africa, especially Kwame Anthony Appiah (*DVRC*, 56–58). He concludes that cultural relevance alone is not enough to justify keeping "traditional rulers" in place when it comes to governance at any level in the continent. Failure to abolish "traditional kingship" leads to a diminution in our aspiration to republicanism, "the political philosophy whose basic tenet is the belief that sovereignty derives ultimately from the people, not from God or other supernatural forces, nor from some hereditary institution or principle" (*DVRC*, 59). As "nearly all African nation states today proclaim themselves republics" (*DVRC*, 59), it stands to reason that the persistence of traditional kingship in them diminishes this aspiration if it does not negate it.

Like Oladosu, I, too, look forward to the day when chieftaincy will not even feature in our discourse of governance or its practice in any part of Africa—nay, the world. But we differ in our justification for it. He, however, remains the only other philosopher to take this position, and his work deserves serious engagement for this reason.

So far, we have considered the views of some African thinkers regarding whether to continue to accommodate chieftaincy in liberal regimes that dominate the African political landscape both as fact and as aspiration at the present time. As Oladosu points out, if our countries were not claiming to be "republics" (in his case), or striving to emplace liberalism-inflected political systems marked by the core tenets of modern political philosophy (in mine), the problem of the place of chieftaincy would not have arisen. Eswatini, for one, does not have this problem. On the contrary, the problem is becoming quite relevant, if not urgent, in Morocco. While the thinkers named here raise concerns that indicate that all is not well with chieftaincy and liberalism, none of them, including Oladosu, have posed the problem posed by chieftaincy and liberalism in terms of Africa's struggle with installing modern liberal-representative democracy in most of the countries that comprise it.

Modernity and Chieftaincy

One reason the problem of the place of chieftaincy eludes scholars is that they do not take seriously the problem's genealogy. The specific concatenation of the problem at hand is circumscribed by modernity. Only if we construe it this way can we make sense of the specific presentation of the issue of chieftaincy. Certainly, chieftaincy has a long genealogy in the history of governance in society, having served humanity for thousands of years as the dominant form of social and political organization across the globe. With the emergence of modernity and its peculiar philosophical anthropology and ethical ontology, the very foundations of the hierarchies typified by chieftaincy were upended. Even where chieftaincy has survived in modern settings its legitimating grounds have shifted and are no longer traceable to those that for a long time undergirded it. I am arguing that it was the irruption into different parts of the continent of this new mode of organizing life and thought and legitimating forms of rule and hierarchies—be it under Christian or Islamic inspiration, or under colonialism—that fostered the problem that we are seeking to make sense of. I have called this an unfinished business of colonialism because it was a big causative element, and the successors to the colonial state, especially the philosophers and other theorists, did not work out ways to harmonize these conflicting inheritances postindependence. The challenge is whether and how chieftaincy can adequately accommodate the core elements of liberalism while preserving its basic character, and whether and how liberalism can accommodate the exigencies of chieftaincy without giving up much of what makes it what it is.[22]

One unpromising way of addressing the problem under review is to escape into definitions. Of course, we know that liberalism has many denominations, if I may be permitted to use a religious analogy. And given the antiquity of chieftaincy, as well its global spread, it is obvious that, short of an unhelpful essentialism, no definition on offer is likely to avail us.[23] Yet, as important as context is, especially when we speak of chieftaincy, it is no less crucial that we offer some elucidations of the core concepts of our discussion.

Notwithstanding the varieties of chieftaincy across the globe, there are certain characteristics that are frequently associated with the idea. Chieftaincy always incorporates some idea of hierarchy whereby no chief is held to be inferior to, under the control of, or equal with those over whom she is chief. In other words, however a chieftaincy is constituted, a chief is always superior to a nonchief; and nonchiefs are expected, prima facie, to defer to the authority of the chief. This hierarchy is without prejudice to how the chieftaincy is constituted. Although there are cases of elective chieftaincies,[24] it has more often been the case that chieftaincies are status-inflected hierarchies dominated by heredity. Even in cases where the original grant came from merit in war or in other areas of life, heredity eventually becomes the single most important requirement for succession over time. In other words, heredity seems to play a central role in the constitution of chieftaincies in many parts of the world. In other areas, at different times, chieftaincy was based on religion, as with popes and caliphs, not to talk of emperors and other potentates. In many religious traditions, sacerdotal titles, too, are inherited and honored as such by those whom they bind. Again, elector eligibility is always restrictive.

Even in our day, in democracies (e.g., the United States), we have the appointment of "czars" for particular exigencies, and such appointments usually entail deferral to such appointees by those who have to work with them. Concomitantly, such appointees are often spared all the "red tape"—tight reporting requirements, superintendence by elected representatives, not to mention having to earn the office concerned through the consent of the governed—that ordinary appointments require of their appointees in the performance of their duties. Pilots, fire chiefs, ship captains, and similar officeholders are seldom required to defer to or consult with their inferiors in certain functions of their offices. Chefs exercise a firm grip on their kitchens and do not routinely submit their choices to vetting or authorization by their inferiors.

It may be objected that we have drawn the boundaries of chieftaincy too broadly and bunched together diverse phenomena that may not be, as a commentator put it, "tokens of the same type." But, as the same commentator concedes, synthesizing a concept of chieftaincy from the presence of what Wittgenstein called "family resemblances" may enable us do better theoretically, as I hope to do here, than if we go the way of the more empirical disciplines that we have elected to avoid. I insist that the convergences that we have identified do fall under this category. I do not wish to suggest, much less affirm, identity.

There is no reason to believe that chieftaincy is, on the face of it, excluded from the contemporary context that is dominated by modernity and its associated ideologies, practices, institutions, and processes. As was just mentioned, it is in seeing how power is allotted and wielded by modern analogues of chieftaincy that we can begin to identify some of the differentiae between chieftaincy and liberalism. We give police chiefs, airline pilots, ship captains, and others wide discretionary powers that often, especially in emergencies, include total control over situations and subordinates. By the same token, such figures frequently overrule their subordinates and command their acquiescence, acceptance, and obedience.

The problem of chieftaincy raises the most concern in politics when it comes to determining the distribution and exercise of political power in a polity. And it is in the modern age and in the evolution and institutionalization of its preferred, dominant mode of rule and political theory, liberalism, that the question of chieftaincy is the thorniest. One of the heralds of modernity was its challenge to and ultimate overthrow of a form of rule that most closely resembled what we would call "chieftaincy"—the divine-ordainment theory. In many monarchies, divine ordainment and heredity, especially primogeniture, determined who ruled and who the successors were. We may take the fact that people obeyed the directives of hereditary rulers certified by God as an index of the people's consent to, or at least acquiescence in, such rule. From ancient times, across the globe, the principle was the same. The ancients in Greece were not democratic, nor were the Egyptians or the Sumerians. Even when the source was elective or merit-based, heredity eventually kicked in. And the boundaries of merit were tightly circumscribed: wealth, bravery, family connections; not the sheer fact of being human and a citizen.

The coming of modernity inaugurated a new form of legitimacy for political rule: governance by consent, a cornerstone of the political theory of liberalism.[25] This is just one element of the complex of ideas that define modernity. In its beginnings, liberalism was forged in city-states and republics dominated by rulers who were not exactly installed by the consent of the governed, as Skinner makes clear. But the fundamental metaphysics of the self, characteristic of modernity, had begun to take root: the principle of subjectivity and its concomitant prohibitions. A fundament of modernity had been the overthrow of status-inflected hierarchies, whether those be rooted in heredity, revelation, or tradition, or in elections in which the offices were not open to all.

No one would deny that the founding principles of chieftaincies across many African societies are like the ones we just adumbrated. What this means is that, if we are not to embrace a static view of African societies and we are not dominated by the metaphysics of difference, we should find it implausible to assume that there were no debates about these founding principles, especially in our more advanced societies. To think that how our modes of governance are right now, or were, say, when they came under colonial control in the nineteenth century, is the way they have always been should scandalize any scholar worth their salt. Indeed, the tragedy is that serious, sophisticated studies of our systems of governance, especially their philosophical grounds, have been preempted by this easy assumption regarding their unchanging nature.

If, for instance, as Mahmood Mamdani argues, chieftaincy, in being incorporated into the colonial system of governance, was profoundly altered, the proper response ought to have been serious engagements with and investigations of what has become of it and its relevance at the present time. And this ought to be done, instead of, as is the wont in African studies, treating chieftaincies as emblems of African identity and, therefore, unproblematic presences in our contemporary situation. No thanks to this attitude, we are never exercised by their nondemocratic provenance, by their incongruousness with new criteria of citizenship and political legitimacy. Some societies, including African ones—e.g., Guinea, Tunisia, Libya, Egypt, Ethiopia, Kenya, Tanzania, Senegal, Côte d'Ivoire, Madagascar—have elected to do away with chieftaincy, tout court, and we have no evidence that their political fortunes have suffered any significant drawbacks on account of this.

In the modern setting, in place of chieftaincy, was substituted the merit principle, premised on the sovereignty of the subject possessed of Reason and capable of improving herself for purposes of world-making and remaking. Government was self-governance writ large. Ultimately, it became definitive of modern governance that no one should be bound by any authority to which he or she has not consented. No government is legitimate unless it has been chartered by the governed. This is a core claim of liberalism, found in all of its many iterations. As we have seen above, one significant implication of the doctrine of governance by consent is that governors are limited by what their constitutors are willing to accept. That is, government is always limited by the charter to which those who legitimated it are committed. This limits government's discretionary powers to the barest minimum, and all the almost pedestrian prohibitions that are emblematic of the modern liberal regime emanate from this simple source. Certainly, if I did not think that life led under such a regime moved us closer to what is most compatible with our nature as free beings, I would not be so exercised by the problem posed by chieftaincy to liberalism.

One way of demarcating the age of chieftaincy from that of modern governance is the fact that in the latter, consent rules and government is limited. And it is not limited by the threat of palace coups, popular insurrection, other contenders to the throne, or religious and sundry ritual taboos. For various societies that enacted the transition to modernity without external intervention or under the rule of another, there were different concatenations of the principle of governance by consent and limited government and prior forms of legitimate rule, some of which involved chieftaincy. While Germany and Italy both became unified countries under chieftaincy, they eventually got rid of it and adopted popular rule based fully on consent. Yet, Britain and the Netherlands, which were part of the original spearhead of modernity in Europe, continue to accommodate chieftaincy in their political setup. Meanwhile, Greece and Spain, later embracers of modernity, split in their preferences: Spain chose to be like the United Kingdom, while Greece adopted the German model. Part of the inspiration for this discussion is my conviction that African countries, too, need to confront the problems posed to their aspiration to realize modern governance (limited and legitimized by the consent of the governed) by the continuing existence of chieftaincy in their polities.

Chieftaincy and Liberalism

If chieftaincy were founded on the consent of the governed and limited in all the ways that a government is limited by the freedom of those it governs to order their lives as they see fit, as long as they do not impair the rights of their fellows to the same, there would be no reason for this work. Most African countries are not marked by these features, and the continuing presence in them of chieftaincy, especially in their political setup, is one reason why we must reflect on the issue of chieftaincy and liberalism. It is why this discussion would be irrelevant in the context of, say, the United States, even though it has a surfeit of chiefs. But these are chiefs without chieftaincies. The case with Native Americans in the United States or First Nations in Canada would be different, though. They have chieftaincies that raise issues like those that exercise us. So do the United Kingdom, the Netherlands, Norway,

Spain, and Thailand, where chieftaincies continue to be integral parts of their modes of governance. In Thailand, for instance, power continues to reside in a god-king, whereas in the United Kingdom, Japan, and other constitutional monarchies, it is said that "the queen or king reigns but does not rule." In some of these nations, it is even plausible to say that their royals' legitimacy is now located not in their bloodlines or tradition but in the popular will. The British Parliament, comprised of representatives of ordinary folks—citizens—now determines who may succeed to the throne, and its acts are required for varying the very boundaries of the monarchy. Spain required a parliamentary vote to restore the monarchy in 1975, whereas the Greeks voted no to a restoration of their monarchy in the same year. For the rest, chiefly power is now beholden to and hemmed in by popular rule determined by elections and the free subject. The same is true of all the other constitutional monarchies chartered under the modern regime.

Here is the problem we are interested in illuminating: What would or should chieftaincy look like in the modern setting? It is posed peculiarly in some of Africa's ex-colonies and at least one in Asia, Malaysia, where colonialists created but never dared—as did the British in India—to solve the question of the relationship between the chieftaincies that used to dominate indigenous modes of governance and the new modes framed by liberalism grounded in modernity. The peculiarity of the African iteration consists in the fact that different potentates dominated different parts of the countries, and there never was a chieftaincy that governed entire countries—except in Morocco,

Ethiopia (a true multinational imperium while it lasted), Libya (a much later development), Eswatini, and Lesotho—or even any single area of particular countries. The closest we have to such dominance was the Sokoto Caliphate, which dominated much of Northern Nigeria, before the country was put together as a single state, and significant parts of today's Niger. This state of affairs has implications for how the problem we are interested in is presented in specific African contexts.

An analogy can be drawn from the Arabian Peninsula and the whole of former Palestine, Transjordan, Syria, Lebanon, and Iraq. Imagine that the various potentates in those areas had been put under a single state in the aftermath of the collapse of the Ottoman Empire. Additionally, imagine that whoever was the superintending power there had fed the illusion that such potentates not only had relevance but had indeed continued to preside over their respective domains. But, then, after independence, citizenship of the new multination state they are now parts of trumps their authority in their respective domains without there having been any serious ideological or philosophical preparing of the ground for the new dispensation. Such a country would have been in the same situation that provoked this discussion of which we are trying to make sense. The respective experiences of the monarchy in Morocco and Libya offer a good illustration of the contrast we are drawing.

At the 1884–85 Berlin West Africa Conference, European imperialist powers cobbled together new African countries that incorporated various previously freestanding states, some with various kinds of chiefs at their helms, others with no discernible chieftaincies in place at all (Liberia was not a chieftaincy but a nominal liberal-democratic republic). Many of those incorporated realms were full-fledged nations, and some of them were colonialists in their own right. Ashanti, Ọ̀yọ́, Sokoto, Dahomey, Buganda, and Kanem-Bornu, to take a few examples, were imperial formations and had vassal states, some of which were outright colonies in some acceptation of that term.

Each was a multinational, multiethnic, multicultural, multilingual formation. On occasion, a national or ethnic group would be dominant, and various smaller or less salient groups would be administered by a single, overlaying, central chieftaincy as the ruling authority. In all the multinational formations, the pattern was that the subordinate units were incorporated by conquest, and this had implications for the grounds of legitimacy for the rule that unfolded in them. As we pointed out earlier, asserting that force was the only basis for their rule is completely mistaken. Studies of these patterns of legitimation in African social formations from a philosophical standpoint are quite rare. What we have, instead, are homogenizations of the chieftaincy form across the continent, as if there were no differences between, say, the Ashantihene in Ghana and the Akirun, the head of the small self-governing kingdom of Ikirun, State of Osun, in Nigeria. The superseded-legitimacy grounds and the problems they pose to the newly constituted, colonialism-inflected governance structures in the new polities across the continent are at the heart of this essay's concerns. Additionally, they incorporate the question of citizenship and political allegiance that has continued to ravage contemporary African states.

Let us go back, briefly, to the two examples we started the book with. We have no reason to think that the Zulu Kingdom, up till the imposition of British colonial rule, did not have stranger, non-Zulu residents within its borders. In other words, however Zulu citizenship was understood or defined, there were non-Zulu who lived under the Zulu chieftaincy. Such residents included immigrants who lived in Zulu cities and towns and villages, and vassals conquered by the Zulu who lived in their own states but were governed by the Zulu state. They obeyed the laws of the state and abided by the principle of social ordering that guided state-individual/individual-individual/group-state/group-individual/group-group interactions within the context of the Zulu kingdom. No doubt, the court of the Zulu king was the locus of ultimate authority regarding governance and how it unfolded in the state as it was then constituted.

Speaking of the same condition that we are dealing with regarding the changes that took place in Ashanti in the relationship between the Ashanti political system and stranger elements that had migrated there, both under colonialism and in its aftermath, Kofi Busia wrote:

> The traditional political system carried with it the corollary that allegiance was personal, not territorial. A man remained a subject of his chief wherever he lived and worked because the ties of kinship remained the same. *Trade and commerce and improved communications have dealt a blow to this tribal conception of citizenship.*

People have travelled from the Northern Territories or the Colony to Ashanti in search of employment. Some of them have settled there more or less permanently. There are many people from these areas who have lived in Ashanti most of their lives, *but they are outside the Ashanti political structure. They are "strangers," no matter how long they live there.*[26]

Meanwhile, unmindful of the problem posed by intra-African migration, we often write as if the biggest migratory movements of Africans were inter-continental. The fact is that there is more internal migration within the continent than emigration from it. Contemporary immigrants who have been the victims of the Zulu king's execration and the violence it engendered are no different, as far as immigrants go, from those who lived under the authority of previous Zulu kings before the independent Zulu nation and its governance passed under the suzerainty, first, of British colonialists and, later, of the contemporary South African state. The difference is that now the Zulu king has immigrants living in areas coincident with what had previously been his predecessors' sphere of authority but who are no longer bound by that authority he continues to think he has. These non-Zulu are mostly other South Africans, some of whom were previously subject to the Zulu king's authority, but now—under the new dispensation, marked by a common supranational South African citizenship—are the king and his fellow Zulu nationals' equals. To add insult to injury, the remainder population (beyond the Zulu and immigrants) is made up of non–South Africans who, under the new dispensation, acquire rights of settlement and to living in Zulu locales regardless of the pleasure or approval of the Zulu king. All that we have said can be applied, with relevant changes, to the Lagos situation, with Rilwan Akiolu and those described by Busia. In the Ghanaian case, non-Ashanti may have remained "strangers" in Ashanti politics, but as Ghanaians they have full rights of Ghanaian citizenship, giving them access to what previously would have been the exclusive preserve of Ashanti citizens.

When these respective states and the kingdoms/empires that chartered them and over which they held sway were incorporated into the new countries, few, if any, efforts were made to confront the philosophical issue of the role of chieftaincy in the putative liberal regimes that were installed in the aftermath of independence from colonial rule. The problem was not originally posed in South Africa, because, at independence, African nations within the South African state were not part of the negotiations; nor were they consulted as to their preferences respecting what place there would be in the new dispensation for chieftaincies that abound in the country.

Before independence, the British colonial authorities, in the name of a dubious indirect-rule policy, had decided to strengthen chieftaincy in indigenous societies regardless of the will of those societies. The template provided apartheid rule in South Africa, post-1948, with the central element of its Bantustan policy, under which so-called tribal homelands, dominated by chiefs who no longer answered to their own people but administered their territories on behalf of South Africa's apartheid rulers, enjoyed pretend autonomy.

In West Africa, where the archimperialist philosopher of "indirect rule," Frederick D. Lugard, held sway, before the colonial administrators took over, the various communities on which indirect rule or its related French equivalent was clamped, were in the throes of significant social change, and had begun debating the position of chiefs in their structures of governance. When British and French colonialists took over, under the philosophical thumbprint of Lugard and Harry Johnston, his cocreator of indirect rule, they sought to reverse these processes, and set about entrenching chieftaincies and extending their reach even to communities that never had them.[27]

This policy was not born of any noble motives. It was dictated by naked racism, under which Africans were not worthy of modern arrangements engendered by the Enlightenment project because, colonial racists insisted, Africans were either not human at all or were such inferior humans that the niceties of modern rule could not have been applicable to their like. Ultimately, with time, "reactive nationalism," as Philip D. Curtin put it, took over, and many Africans embraced chieftaincy as part of their affirmation of self and community in the face of the denial of same by racist colonialists. At no time was there any consensus across the continent that chieftaincies were an unproblematic presence in the new sociopolitical dispensations that were being cobbled together under colonial designs.[28]

The Genesis of the Unfinished Business

For us to understand this peculiar version of the problem of chieftaincy and liberalism in Nigeria and English-speaking West Africa, in general, we need a little history.[29] The bane of much of the discussion of chieftaincy in the literature is its ahistorical nature. It is as if chieftaincy had not only always been there in our various societies, it had also remained the same through time, and whatever happened to it under colonialism were the only change of note with which analysis must deal. This is the root of the persistent false binary in African studies, generally, that opposes "traditional chieftaincy" to "modern governance" inspired by colonialism. This opposition is demonstrably false, for even the simplest mode of governance in what might be a small community that has perdured for any appreciable length of time must have a history marked by changes in its structures, if not its founding principles. When the focus turns to some of the states spread across the continent, especially in north and west Africa, we must reject summarily any analysis that assumes that the way they were taken to be when colonialism began to mess with them was no different from how they were when they were first chartered.

For example, the chieftaincy associated with the Sokoto Caliphate was of eighteenth-century provenance and was inspired by developments within Islam and its governance template, combined with local Fulbe\Pula\ Peul\Fulani inspiration. I remain befuddled by how scholars who celebrate D. T. Niane's *Sundiata* as an embodiment of "traditional" lore persistently miss the repeated references to and adulation of Alexander the Great in the text, or the fact that the king was domesticated in Mandingo;[30] not to speak of the attempt to trace Sundiata's legitimacy to Islam's founder. What this means is that the chieftaincy that the French dealt with in what they termed "Soudan français" and the Mali that eventually emerged from it had more "foreign" accretions than the moniker "traditional ruler" could accommodate; and its history is a lot more complex. Additionally, the Sokoto Caliphate that Lugard mastered in 1903 was an Islamic emporium, not a "traditional Fulani" rulership. These historical details hold deep implications for our idea of the grounds of legitimacy of these states and why their subjects embraced an obligation to obey the rules that emanated from them while they lasted.

The Benin Kingdom, too, had dynastic histories going back more than half a millennium by the time it made its recorded initial acquaintance with Portuguese adventurers, at the close of the fifteenth century.[31] Even if the Benin monarchy had stopped evolving at that point in time, it would still have meant that the monarchy that was overthrown in 1897 could not have answered easily to the tag "traditional rule." "Traditional" does not open the space of analysis and historicity, a tracking of the many iterations of tradition and its evolution through time and the many accretions that settle within it. That is, any serious engagement with the Benin monarchy must reckon with its historicity and acknowledge its evolution over time regarding its constitution, its governing principles, and the changes such have undergone. Additionally, many instances of chieftaincy that we call "traditional" now were manufactured in the twentieth century from whole cloth, by colonial authorities who were convinced that modernity-inflected governance-by-consent was not appropriate for Africans, even if Africans wanted it. Let us substantiate the claims just made.

History is of vital importance here. We go back to the nineteenth century. The early nineteenth century witnessed in West Africa the second wave of Christian evangelization. This was simultaneous with the abolition of slavery and the European slave trade. These twin developments had epochal consequences for life and thought in the region, both for people and institutions. As a direct consequence of the rapine associated with the slave trade, many societies had been thrown into turmoil and lives and institutions upended. The coming of the first cohort of this wave of evangelizers, Protestants for the most part, was marked by their commitment to the rejuvenation of African agency and to making Africa able, once again, to govern itself and move in tandem with the world in humanity's march of progress. But the template from which this great future was to be fashioned was forged from modernity. The core tenets of modernity, with their roots going back to the Renaissance and the Reformation in Europe, the conquest of the Americas and the contestations over land and life with Native Americans and First Nations, and the Haitian Revolution, were the guiding principles that this first cohort of second-wave evangelizers, most of whom were themselves Africans, sought to realize in their efforts at remaking African societies. The identity of this cohort of evangelizers made all the difference, and they, ultimately, were the original vector of modernity in this region of Africa.

The historical conjuncture that resulted from the processes just described intensified the destabilizing of settled social relations that had been underway with the ravages of the European slave trade for close to three centuries. The importance of this history cannot be overemphasized. Different polities in West Africa did not all take part in the transatlantic slave trade (TAST) with the same intensity. And there can be no doubt that there must be implications for life and thought in those that were deeply involved in the trade. TAST involved significant metaphysical presuppositions as well as ethical principles that determined who could be sold or kept as a slave and when it was improper to hold someone as a slave internally, much less sell them to unknown climes. We know, for instance, that the Kingdom of Dahomey was an absolute creation of the TAST and was, to all intents and purposes, a slave state.[32] By contrast, for a long time the Ọ̀yọ́ Empire thrived on raiding and selling others who were not its citizens or otherwise culturally protected vassals within the context of a shared historico-cultural Yorùbá identity. The incursion by Fulani jihadists in the eighteenth century, rather late in the trade and just before the abolitionist tide turned on it, eventually undermined this internal arrangement, and this coincided with an influx of Ọ̀yọ́ Yorùbá slaves late in the trade that explains the preponderance of this specific cultural group in Brazil and Cuba and the subsequent survival of the relevant culture in those places till now.

Chieftaincy as a mode of governance determined the contours of citizenship or subjecthood in those polities. At the head of those structures within which the criteria of eligibility for enslavement were set and executed sat chiefs whose powers and legitimacy began to fray with the increasing social dislocation caused by the intensity of the heinous trade over time. One such institution that was vulnerable to radical change because of these developments was the mode of governance. As A. I. Asiwaju points out,

> The nineteenth-century wars in the western half of the area from the Mono to the Niger produced far-reaching population shifts and demographic changes. ... Within the affected West African localities themselves, socio-political changes of revolutionary character also took place, occasioned by massive population movements.[33]

In the specific case of the Yorùbá territory, Asiwaju avers,

> The wars and their social effects culminated in the development of a new society; and this gave rise to the need to fashion new methods and styles of government. The new situation made for the

emergence of warriors as dominant class and the eclipsing of the pre-existing monarchical class. This is particularly true of the Yoruba area where the *obas* lost control to the *baloguns* or warlords. The experiments with military dictatorship in Ijaiye under Kurumi, federalism in Abeokuta under Sodeke and constitutional monarchy in Epe under Kosoko illustrate the efforts in nineteenth-century Yorubaland to fashion new constitutions appropriate for the political management of the new society generated by the wars.[34]

Colonialism had not become a factor in these processes.

I argue that epochal changes were afoot in the grounds of political governance. Many erstwhile settled political regimes, mostly chieftaincies in which there was an admixture of heredity and divine ordainment—from city-states to multination-states like the Ọyọ Empire, to theocracies like Sokoto and Segu-Tucolor—joined by the rare elective chieftaincies (for example, the Fanti), were all in the process of being shaken, dismantled, and reconstituted. Social hierarchies that had, for the most part, been founded on gender, age, religion, ethnicity, nationality, and so on, were being torn down by what Lamin Sanneh has styled "antistructure."[35] The dominant instance that was under severe strain, with some of it disintegrating, was chieftaincy. It was not just the strain caused by the social disruption engendered by the violence associated with the TAST.

The most important point here is that the TAST disrupted the structures of governance in the areas it affected. If what we said about the historicity of all formations is granted, it follows that there is no reason to believe that other African societies were not undergoing their own strains and stresses caused by other factors, endogenous or exogenous. For instance, the late eighteenth century was the occasion for various constitutional experiments in the West African Sahel under the inspiration of Islamic socioreligious movements that altered the governance landscape from Senegambia to Sudan. The Mfecane movement led eventually to the consolidation of the Zulu under Shaka, the dispersion of the Zulu to present-day Zimbabwe, and changes in the governance structures of many areas in southern Africa. The notion that these were static chieftaincies that were recast by colonialism could not be further from the truth.

Of equal, if not greater, significance is the strain caused by the social change that was afoot in many locations due to the presence of foreign elements, of new ways of thinking and organizing social life. Although not widespread, small Christian and Muslim communities could be found in many African societies. In many areas, as we pointed out above, Islam had become the source of legitimacy for local polities that had altered sufficiently for them to be constituted on, to say the least, hybrid foundations. In others, new challenges were being mounted to indigenous modes of governance by newly constituted groups made rich by participation in international trade.

Chief among the most disruptive change agents in West and South Africa were those African graduates of what I call the missionary school of modernity. Among their ranks, there were internal debates regarding how to remake themselves and their societies in light of their newly acquired templates for social living and social ordering. Many of them were either formerly enslaved persons who had repatriated from the New World or "recaptives," who were destined for slavery but had been saved by the British Navy on the high seas and resettled in Freetown, whence many of them wended their way to their original homelands in various West African countries, especially Nigeria and Ghana.

Some of these new Christians regarded their own capture for the slave trade as part of a divine plan to introduce them to "civilization," at the time a synonym for post-Reformation Christianity. They regarded it as a mandate from God to remake their society in the Christian (modern) image. For some of them, chieftaincy was inseparable from the system that victimized them by selling them into slavery, and thus the legitimizing grounds of that structure and the hierarchies built on it held no more attraction for them. Those status-inflected hierarchies that had also been weakened by the social dislocations caused by slave raiding and civil strife became prime candidates for subversion by a new elite made up of Christian converts for whom modernity was an attractive replacement for their erstwhile foundational principles, institutions, and even modes of social living.[36]

In the British possessions, there were debates among these groups regarding what to do with chieftaincies. Such debates predated the imposition of formal colonialism. Even in places like present-day Ghana, informal colonialism barely touched the operations of chieftaincies, and the questions asked concerning them were raised by indigenes themselves. They did not flinch from the challenges posed by the new, of which they were products and harbingers, to the old, which they could see was badly shaken, overthrown in certain cases, and definitely no longer as assertive or dominant as before. Left to their own designs, just as has always happened in other societies in history, including African societies of the past, African thinkers of the period, too, would have figured out how best to shape their realities in light of inevitable change.

It is unfortunate that the debates among modern African thinkers, activists, and politicians respecting what to do with indigenous modes of governance of whatever kind—chieftaincies or quasi republics—are hardly ever referenced. Yet, not only did these debates predate the imposition of colonial rule, they lasted through the period of colonial rule and persisted in the postindependence period. Some of the political crises that ended up triggering political insta-bility in places like Ghana, Uganda, and Nigeria in the postindependence period turned, in part, on the place of chieftaincies in the newly minted republics putatively grounded in liberal-democratic principles. This is why I suggest that the problem of chieftaincy and liberalism is an unfinished business of colonialism. I shall have more to say about this presently.

In the debates conducted by modern Africans regarding what to do with their old ways in the face of new ways of organizing life and thought, four possibil-ities are discernible.

1. They could decide to shun the new and keep the old unchanged. Here we may find nodes on which to build a study of a modern conservative tendency in African social and political thought. A good example of this tendency would be William Esuman-Gwira Sekyi (Kobina Sekyi) and his spirited defense of old

Africa against the ravages of a modernity that he thought hewed too much to Westernization and\or Europeanization.

2. They could keep the old but modify it, taking care to determine by how much and in what direction. Again, we have very good examples of this tendency. Indeed, one could argue that this was the dominant tendency, and it was reflected in the arguments and practical efforts of African apostles of modernity to renew their societies along modern lines. James Africanus Beale Horton, Samuel Ajayi Crowther, J. E. Casely Hayford, John Mensah Sarbah, Ọbafemi Awolowo, Leopold Sédar Senghor, and others fall within this category. The efforts of the Fanti Confederation to create a constitutional monarchy and the futile attempt by George W. Johnson to recast Egba native governance in the late nineteenth century under the auspices of the Egba United Board of Management are clear attempts at constitutional reform in those polities.

3. They could accept the new wholesale and, however implausible it may sound, extirpate the old and its meanings for them. Implausible, because, as we now know all too well from the history of revolutions, no wholesale extirpation ever occurs in history; the rhetoric usually claims more than the reality can justify. I do not know of any examples of this, but that does not mean future research will not turn up any.

4. They could accept the new with modifications, determining by how much and in what direction. In the twentieth century, the late emperor Haile Selassie decided to modernize the Ethiopian judiciary by adopting elements of the Scottish judicial tradition.

Back in the nineteenth century, we have evidence of similar, motley borrowings by Africans from their European and non-European partners and conquerors. Many chieftaincies in Yorùbá states have in their ranks titles of Islamic/Fulani/Hausa inspiration, and chieftaincies created in churches and mosques mirror Yorùbá hierarchies, especially in the allocation of statuses.

One thing is indisputable, in the area of governance: African converts to modernity, along with their sympathizers and allies within the indigenous governance structures, were exercised by the need to update their modes of governance, and their model was incontrovertibly some form or other of that suggested by what we know as liberalism. Thus did they inaugurate the question of how liberal governance should relate to the issue of chieftaincy in a post-evangelization, post-slavery, and, ultimately, for us, postindependence world. At least, that was what they thought. What they did not anticipate, much less reckon with, was the imposition of a harsh, anti-Black-racism-inflected colonialism that would put paid to those ambitions and strip African subjects of any say in the evolution of their societies and their pertinent institutions.

Colonialism Intervenes: Arrested Development

Things began to change for the worse as the nineteenth century wore on and various parts of Africa went from informal empire, where local communities were under nominal control by chartered companies, to being declared "protectorates" and colonies and passed on to colonial administrators. One principal justification for ending rule by commercial concerns by the British, to limit ourselves to just one example, and imposing formal colonialism was that the chartered companies were very inefficient at what they did, and their increasing reliance on and deployment of British military forces meant commitments that the government assumed for purposes that it did not control. Additionally, it was held that the subject peoples needed to be brought to modernity, the undergirding philosophy of the age that had transformed Europe itself.

The administrators who supplanted the missionaries and the traders, the real engine of colonial rule, were initially welcomed by the African moderns. Again, we limit ourselves to British West Africa. Africans initially believed the colonialists' proclamation of their desire to bring Africans to modernity, and updating the mode of governance was an important element of that promise. Of course, at that time, African moderns had no reason to doubt those they regarded as their tutors in the ways of modernity—a new European cohort of missionaries, traders, and administrators—were in any significant way different from an earlier cohort that was committed to strengthening African agency and putting it at the head of the movement for change in the region. They discovered that their new partners were products of a Europe where racism was becoming rife and the humanity of Africans and their capacity for improvement were increasingly objects of doubt, if not outright denial. This was the beginning of the nationalist struggle against colonialism, and the Africans, even as they continued to see their future as independent subjects of the British Empire, did not accept to play second fiddle to overbearing colonial administrators.

No, they were not accepting of racially inflected status when we speak of their continuing to see their future as independent subjects—as citizens were then called—of the British Empire. But, because they were accepting of modernity's core tenets, and saw themselves as citizens (i.e., fellow charterers) of the polis made up of the British Empire, even as they remained, culturally, African nationals, they were comfortable with seeking similar status for a Western African federation as was bestowed on Canada and Australia. What is even more remarkable was how some of them insisted that, despite the traditions of particularism represented in their respective ethnicities, they constituted a nation, and it was this nation, they envisioned, that would replace the multiple kingdoms and emporia dotted across West Africa at the time. This position was quite consistent with their initial openness to curtailing the reach of chieftaincy in their societies. Only when colonial racism forced a reactive nationalism on them did they begin to tout chieftaincy's identitarian element, while never considering it a worthy alternative to modern consent-based governance. That is, their defense of chieftaincy was as a cultural artifact, not a preferred regime.

The most serious breach at that point in time was a result of the Africans' desire to install modern states founded on liberal principles and colonial administrators' insistence on restoring failed chieftaincies and strengthening others in ways that were not even consonant with indigenous principles of legitimacy. This is why our analysis cannot be indifferent to history. Internal debates within various African communities, social change in many others, and political upheavals and associated constitutional experiments meant that any attempt to designate any particular form of chieftaincy as "the true model" for any of those societies was a falsehood. It was the imposition of what I have elsewhere called "sociocryonics": "the ignoble science of cryopreserving social forms, arresting them and denying them and those whose social forms they are the opportunity of deciding what, how, and when to keep any of their social forms."[37] It was the preemption of African debates and initiatives regarding the place of chieftaincy in the emergent polities of Africa in the nineteenth century and the imposition by the newly dominant colonial administrators of chieftaincy on various African spaces and peoples in the early twentieth century that inaugurated the problem that we still are trying to solve well into the third decade of the twenty-first century. Lagos and Calabar, for instance, witnessed the first local-council elections outside the purview and jurisdiction of local chieftains in 1904; analogous events took place in Accra in 1920.

If what I have just said is true, or at least plausible, then all who talk about chieftaincy as if it were a question of African identity, a necessary part of governance in Africa, or an unproblematic inheritance that was distorted by colonialist shenanigans, the effects of which are to be rolled back by its revival and reintegration into governance at the present time, must address the case we make here. I hope to have given sufficient reason for why I insist that this is an unfinished business of colonialism.

Where, prior to the imposition of formal colonialism, the African moderns embraced the idea of progress and were ready to alter their indigenous institutions and practices according to the dictates of the new way of life they had favored, their colonial administrators elected for and imposed sociocryonics on African communities. The way in which colonial administrators peremptorily stopped the movement toward redefining the modes of governance in many African polities is a quintessential instance of sociocryonics. The facticity of chieftaincy is always assumed by commentators; the question of its historicity is hardly ever raised, except to talk of how it was affected by colonialism. The internal debates over its place in governance in many of our polities are never referenced much less engaged. Progress requires that we take these debates very seriously.

The colonial authorities preempted progress. They decided that Africans were not the type of people who could either adopt or benefit from modernity and its associated processes, practices, and institutions. There is no area where the impact of sociocryonics is more direct and starker or more impactful than in governance and its many modes. No doubt, there were changes afield in this area in the nineteenth century among several African communities, from Ethiopia to South Africa, from Senegambia to Egypt. In West Africa, Africans, including recaptives and returnees, were struggling both conceptually and in practice to determine what would be the best form of governance and which enabling philosophical principles would undergird it. Africa in the nineteenth century was a beehive of constitutional experimentation. I have written above of at least two such experiments—the Fanti Confederation and the Egba United Board of Management—that were set to indigenize the debates and structures of liberalism, even while they creatively worked to adapt chieftaincies in their respective areas into the new proposed structures. To offer a third example, in the same period Ibadan introduced a new governing arrangement where merit—especially in war—determined who had power, and heredity played no role. Even though the arrangement was couched in the language of chieftaincy, Ibadan infused the relevant terms with new significance.

Why is this important? Ibadan is the kind of example that not merely merits scrutiny and sophisticated analysis but is sure to challenge the pat application of the tag "traditional" to all things African in contradistinction to what has been considered modern or influenced by colonialism. Ibadan was not, repeat, not an iteration of the regular mode of governance in Yorùbá history up till its emergence. On the contrary, it was a new understanding of rule and legitimacy based on merit, even if that merit was determined by or anchored in success at war, mastery in brigandage, and ability to create and sustain large followership. That the arrangement was couched in chiefly language has more to do with the limits imposed by the then-available models and less to do with replicating existing traditions of rule. Of course, it might be objected that Ibadan did not need to go the way of having an ọba, given that it was then still under the suzerainty, even if nominal, of the crumbling Ọ̀yọ́ Empire.

What is of moment here is that the entire setup of rule in Ibadan was novel. I contend that, had the experiment been allowed to evolve organically, it might have become a unique example of a chieftaincy, if it was that, that was open to all without the heavy hand of heredity, tradition, or religion determining eligibility. This interpretation is supported by the fact that Ibadan was also a center of evangelization, home to some of the most significant members of the class of African graduates of the missionary school of modernity, who were desirous of seeing Ibadan lead the charge to remake Yorùbá society in the modern image. Its leading lights formed themselves into the Ẹgbẹ́ Àgbà Ò Tán (literally "Elders-Are-Not-Extinct Society"), whose founding instruments showed clearly their desire to modify, radically, the structure of life and thought in their locality.[38]

As in similar cases across the continent, colonialism put paid to this ambition. We ended up with an indirect-rule distortion of this experiment that would eventually lead to Ibadan, in the 1980s, becoming one with what is standardly interpreted as the Yorùbá mode of governance, with the gift of a crown to its "ọba," a moniker that did not emerge from Ibadan but was handed out in 1936 by the colonial administrators.

The colonial administrators were having none of our moderns' preferences. Sociocryonics put paid to the ambitions of Africans to alter their modes of rule to reflect new influences, especially when it came to answering such central questions of political philosophy as Who ought to rule when not all can rule? And what limits are to be imposed on the exercise of power when it comes to the relationship between the individual and the state? As far as I know, rarely do African philosophers conduct their political-philosophy discourse in the African context in terms of the central questions of political philosophy. For the most part, it is almost as if pedigree is enough to justify the advocacy of any preferred mode of governance. For those who wish to defend the continuing relevance of chieftaincy, the argument is founded on the supposed incompatibility between "Western" liberal democracy built on modernity and African modes of governance undergirded by tradition. Even those who are opposed to chieftaincy tend to appeal more to pragmatic difficulties associated with the career of liberal democracy in Africa than to philosophical issues with it. Yet, we must not make light of the contributions of thinkers like Ọbafẹmi Awolowo, who is almost alone in insisting that, in contemporary Africa, no status-derived office should be superior to elective offices in the polity. And when he had charge of a region in Nigeria, he subordinated the authority of chiefs to that of elected officials, in a clear reversal of the preferences of Nigeria's former British colonial overlords.[39] Kwame Nkrumah and Julius Nyerere, too, were thinkers who embraced liberal-democratic theory and held that chieftaincies must be made subordinate to elective offices.[40]

Under the inspiration of modern liberal theory, many African theorists wished to replace the rule of chiefs with the rule of the educated elite, which was to be based on the equality of all before the law, the rule of law, the separation of powers, and the consent of the governed as expressed through free and fair elections, as well as the sovereignty of the individual. Even when the theorists sought, as most did, to combine the best of the old with the best of the new, one thing was central to their plans: the preference for elective offices open to everyone who met certain qualifications, and definitely not determined by ascription, be that heredity, tradition, military prowess, wealth, or religion. Some were even open to preserving chieftaincy for the sake of having a unifying political figurehead, shorn of power over the direction of everyday executive functions, along the lines of British constitutional monarchy. In other words, chieftaincy would be redesigned and put on new footing. Chiefs would be nothing like chiefs that Africans were used to.

Since the time the colonial administrators won out, the course of the political history of the region was set, and the movement toward modern liberal-representative government was stymied. In many areas, chieftaincy was strengthened by the colonial authorities and was used as an antidote to what the administrators regarded as the poison of educated elite influence on the direction of political evolution in the colonies and protectorates.[41] Even more egregious was the fact that many chieftaincies had more powers vested in them than were provisioned for in their original indigenous establishment. In Nigeria, for instance, many groups that never had chieftaincies as part of their indigenous modes of governance were saddled with artificial chieftaincies crafted by colonial administrators.[42] The administrators' justification was that, given the backwardness—nonexistence, even—of African humanity, rule by chiefs, and strong ones at that, was the only viable option for African governance. The protests of African moderns did not matter; they were contemptuously dismissed as pathological mimics who wished to be Europeans and could not be counted as "authentic" representatives of African ways of being human.

Crucially, it was in this context of the new colonial administrators tinkering with indigenous modes of governance that the problem of chieftaincy and liberalism was birthed. But even here we must not assume that this was the case for every part of the continent. Part of what I hope a work like this does is to shake us out of our complacency toward received wisdom regarding using Africa as a unit of analysis. When I cite examples from different parts of Africa, it is not with the intention of homogenizing realities or generalizing across the continent. I cite such examples only when they offer corroboration of the theoretical or philosophical point at stake, or a departure from the same. There is widespread acceptance that colonial administrators—be they French, English, Portuguese, or, much more briefly, German or Italian—profoundly affected the fortunes and character of chieftaincy, and those changes have perdured pretty much to the present.

What I fail to see in the literature is an appreciation of the complexities of different societies before they fell victim to the ravages of European colonialism. As we have pointed out repeatedly in this discussion, in much of West Africa dominated by British colonialism, the impact of social changes engendered by the European slave trade and its aftermath, followed by the introduction of modernity and its tenets by Christian missionaries (dominated for however so brief a time by African agency), had begun to chip away at the legitimacy and the very structure of chieftaincy in some parts. In others, social changes occasioned by developments in Islam and its propagation around the northern and western parts of the continent had thrown up new modes of governance that colonial administrators had to confront.

Between those Africans who wanted to remake their societies along modern lines and those desirous of installing theocracies, the colonial administrators did not have a clear deck to build on. What is more, in many African societies, the prestige of chieftaincy had suffered severe blows, quite a few nearly to the point of death. Of course, both British and French colonialists did not want to pay the full cost of empire, especially when it came to their African imperial adventures. What they did was to reinvent chieftaincy where it was moribund, manufacture it from whole cloth where it was not on the ground, revive it where it was dead, and strengthen it where it still held sway. In making these fateful choices, the colonialists paid no attention whatsoever to the preferences of the natives. And because of their racism, they could not bring themselves to work with that segment of the native population that was already inducted into modernity and had embraced its core tenets concerning modes of governance. This group would not acquiesce in what they regarded, good moderns that they were, as illegitimate rule—it was not based on the consent of the governed, for one thing—and they duly challenged the colonial administrators.

Whether it was the moderns or operators of native institutions of governance who also questioned the legitimacy of colonial rule, the administrators responded with violence. This was not a mere pragmatic response. It emanated from their white-supremacist ideology, which encased Africans in the metaphysics of difference. A. I. Asiwaju has argued that this rule by force and illegality was standard fare for Africa's European colonizers, even as his focus was on the French in West Africa. Africa's colonizers deployed "structural violence" to solve what they styled "the Native Problem"—a euphemism for native resistance to colonialism—ranging from pretend legal restraints like "the Seditious Offences Ordinance of 1909 which sought to ban agitations and criticisms against the government of Southern Nigeria," which, incidentally, was where indirect rule faced the stiffest challenge from the graduates of the missionary school of modernity, to setting up "local African aristocracies, which functioned, often despotically, as agents of the colonial administration."[43]

In German territories, shared between France and Britain at the end of World War I, administration through coercion was dated to a decree of the Imperial Chancellor of 25 April 1896, which authorized in Togo and Cameroon a crude form of repression involving arbitrary imprisonment and free use of the whip for petty offences. In Portuguese and Belgian colonies, the *"regime do indigenato"* and the policy of "paternalism" respectively were operated along lines which were identical both in theory and practice with the French Indigénat regime. In all these contexts, administration by coercion was officially conceived as a means to an end and not an end in itself.[44]

Frederick D. Lugard and the Reconfiguration of Chieftaincy

Now we present the core ideas on chieftaincy originated by Frederick D. Lugard, which continue to
operate in Nigeria, for the most part, sixty years after
independence. Lugard's principal claim to fame was his
work in northern Nigeria as part of the expeditionary
force that subdued the Sokoto Caliphate for the
British Royal Niger Company, in 1903. In his *Political
Memoranda: Revision of Instructions to Political Officers
on Subjects Chiefly Political and Administrative, 1913–
1918*, in "Memo No. IX.—Native Administration,"
Lugard reconfigured the idea of chieftaincy and forced
it on British colonies across the continent. It needs be
borne in mind that Lugard turned the caliphate system
into the model of native rule because he preselected
the Fulani rulers of the Sokoto Caliphate as "natural
rulers," because he found them to be "the most
advanced race" among "black Africans." He styled his

system "Indirect Rule, viz., rule through Native Chiefs, who are regarded as an integral part of the machinery of Government, with well-defined powers and functions recognized by Government and by law, and not dependent on the caprice of an Executive Officer."[45]

This declaration looks simple and nonthreatening enough. In reality, with indirect rule, potentates in their own right, with authority limited only by the constitutional provisions of their original charter in their domains, became subordinate agents of a superior power, legitimated by nothing but the say-so of the British colonial governor, unless restrained by the colonial secretary. Following this proclamation, Lugard declared that "the Native Chiefs thus recognized were not to be regarded as *independent rulers*. They were the *delegates of the Governor* whose representative was the Resident" (*PM*, 297; my emphasis).[46] Later, in section 16, he was very explicit that the chiefs, under this dispensation, were no more than civil servants. Citing the observation of his successor, Sir P. Girouard, with approval, he averred:

> I have observed (writes Sir P. Girouard—Memo. 27, para. 4) a tendency in some directions to impress Emirs with the idea that they are sovereign rulers over independent States. I must strongly insist that such action is most unwise, and might prove disastrous. I have impressed upon Emirs that they are my Wakils in their emirates, but they must be guided by the word of the Resident, who speaks for me. ... If we are to have Native Administration, the use of the Fulani and Kanembu would appear to be inevitable, not as ruling Sovereigns or Princes, but as Governors, which is all they are entitled to claim by their own faith." ...

The title of "Emir"—or "Amir"—indicates that these Head Chiefs, though servants of the Government, amenable to all the laws of Nigeria, and liable to removal in case of treason or other sufficient cause, are the trusted Governors of their "Emirates," and the Government will deal with all Chiefs and peoples subordinate to them solely through their agency.

I lay great stress on the position of the Emir as a "Wakil" or Governor under the Suzerain power, for it is the basis, as my successor rightly perceived, of the whole structure of the Native Administration in Nigeria (*PM*, 303).

Just so no one is left in doubt that this preference for chieftaincy was completely devoid of any respect for the societies or the wishes of the people, Lugard stated that

Section 4. Subject to these limitations it was the declared policy of the Government to restore to the Chiefs the prestige and authority which they had lost by the British conquest, or *forfeited by their own previous mal-administration* (PM, 297; my emphasis).

Recall what we said above about the changes that were taking place on the constitutional front in many societies across the African continent. We have pointed out that in parts of West Africa, especially in Nigeria, there were already moves toward modernity and some efforts at the installation of modern institutions. What is more, in Lagos, which was a colony, there were Africans who were British subjects—as citizens were then called—and these were the same people that Lugard was prepared to force to be under chiefly rule. More remarkably, if, indeed, chiefs had lost "prestige and authority" in part due to "their own mal-administration," why would anyone who was even mildly interested in the fortunes of the governed, someone who claimed to be the product of a modern system of rule, consider, much less impose, policies that were designed to restore such chiefs to prominence?

Be that as it may—with all the consequences that it had on the evolution of the colonial state and the fortunes of modern rule after independence—what is of moment is that, from the time of Lugard's proclamation, chiefs, especially those that could be regarded as "paramount" (that is, previous rulers of their respective domains, such as the Zulu king and the Ọba of Lagos), were no longer so by force of tradition and custom of the respective polity but by two procedures inaugurated by Lugard that persist till today in Nigeria.

First, no one is a chief until their appointment has been published in the government gazette, a publication that tells the public that a certain act or proclamation of government now has the force of law. This was how Lugard put it: "Section 12. A 'Native Authority' is defined as any Chief or other Native so appointed by the Governor, and a 'Recognised Chief' is one whose status has been formally recognized by Government"; that is, it "must be gazetted" (*PM*, 301).

The second novel procedure is the introduction of a staff of office. According to "Section 26. The formal recognition of the position of a 1st or 2nd grade Chief is notified by the presentation of a 'Staff of Office,' and in the case of the former by a Letter of Appointment on a parchment scroll. These appointments are notified in the Gazette" (PM, 307). And there is an oath that they must swear to at their installation, where this staff is formally presented, and the oath was, while colonialism lasted, to the British Queen, and is now to the Nigerian State or its federating units. Even academics are surprised at the recency of the staff as an insignia of office for kings, emirs, and such, who now fancy themselves as potentates but whose status has not broken free from the constrictions of the colonial state that designated them not as such, but only as chiefs. And it does not occur to many of us who write about these issues to problematize the conflict between the self-perception of an ọba, emir, obi, obong, or shehu, across the land and the objective reality, vide the two procedures just mentioned, in which he is a glorified "Wakil" to whoever is, in the present case, elected authority in the contemporary Nigerian state. It is not only the requirements of gazetting and presentation of letters of appointment and staffs of office that persist in the present; it is also that the gradation of chiefs introduced by Lugard remains the framework for assigning status to chiefs across Nigeria.

These procedures have severe implications for chieftaincy as it has come to us at the present time. The imposition of indirect rule in Western Nigeria aborted both a nascent transition to modernity that was underway there as a result of the availability of British citizenship to certain inhabitants of the then colony of Lagos and an experiment in modern self-governance by an independent Egba United Government, the successor to the failed Egba United Board of Management, in Abeokuta, which Lugard termed an "eyesore" and immediately dissolved on becoming the governor-general of an amalgamated Nigeria, in

1914. Given this, it is problematic to continue to write about chieftaincy as if it were not a bone of contention among different constituencies, especially indigenous ones, in our various polities.

If, indeed, custom- and tradition-inflected legitimacy is no longer final or determinant in the constitution and legitimization of chieftaincy—it is not in South Africa or Nigeria—then the continuing assertion of authority in their domains that we saw with Zwelithini and Akiolu is groundless unless, of course, constitutional provisions are made to accommodate chieftaincy in the prevailing aspiring liberal regimes in their respective polities.

Moreover, the very idea of "traditional ruler" may have become outmoded, given that, even after all the relevant rites and observances mandated by the culture of a specific domain are performed, if the appointment is not "gazetted" and a letter of appointment and staff of office are not publicly presented, there is no chief.

These were issues that, had colonialism allowed native agency serious autonomy, might have been resolved in ways that paid attention to the preferences of natives and the evolution of their modes of governance as elements of an organic formation guided by their history and usages. Ibadan, probably, would not have been encumbered with an ọba today had this been the case, and the continual crises of chieftaincy in various domains would have been preempted.

By blocking the direction under native agency of the evolution of political forms, employing structural violence to prop up tottering kingdoms in the western parts of Nigeria, extending the reach of the caliphate to areas in the middle of the country it could not itself subdue, manufacturing chieftaincies in the eastern parts that had not had them, and criminalizing the expression of alternative ideas through sedition ordinances, colonialism ensured that future liberal regimes would have this problem to contend with. In a sense, given the near isomorphism between the colonialism that predominated in much of Africa and chieftaincies in many of them, too, it is not an accident that both are hostile to liberalism.

The Aftermath

At the conclusion of the struggle for independence, Africans were practically left with no choice but to inherit government institutions with chieftaincies as one of the pillars, with little opportunity to consider, much less resolve, the contradictions between chieftaincy (a system built on ascription, authority, tradition or religion, or colonial expediency) and modern governance (built on merit, consent, representation, and popular control). Among the ambivalent and ambiguous legacies of decolonization was a much-attenuated capacity of Africans to choose their rulers and preferred mode of governance.[47] It bequeathed what Mahmood Mamdani has termed "decentralized despotism," the cornerstone of which was chieftaincy that was not quite accountable to the governed, was pretty much unelected, much less representative than liberal regimes, and that is at the core of the two incidents related at the beginning of this essay.

In the contemporary period in Africa, we have a situation in which indigenous governance structures—bastardized, as we just indicated, to the extent that they can no longer be associated with their original moorings, but not exactly nested into new ones inspired by modern liberal-democratic principles—continue to be cogs in the wheels of governance. Unlike in the United Kingdom, where the Queen is only a ceremonial and symbolic presence in the British government, in African countries most successor rulers have in their attempts to determine what to do with chieftaincy in the postindependence period stumbled from one half-baked idea to another. Examples range from the changing fortunes of the Buganda chieftaincy in Uganda under the Milton Obote government to those of the Ashanti version in Kwame Nkrumah's Ghana, the Aláàfin of Ọ̀yọ́ in Western Nigeria even before independence, and the discussions that led to the writing and adoption of the South African Constitution, in 1995.

Some African countries, such as Guinea and Tanzania, did legislate chieftaincy out of existence after independence. Others, like South Africa and Uganda, modified chieftaincy as part of the new constitutional order. In Nigeria, the current constitutional regime does not make any provisions for chieftaincy, but chiefs continue to be part of the structure of governance, especially at the municipal level, hence the Lagos ọba's vituperations. Significantly, most of those chiefs have now been reduced to mayor-like administrative status, if that, and they no longer wield the kind of political power they did before the advent of a liberal-democratic-representative dispensation. The fact that chieftaincy continues to stand out like a sore thumb in a democratic regime points to what, we argue, is an inherent incompatibility between it and liberal democracy.[48]

As we said at the beginning of this discussion, had Goodwill Zwelithini not been the King of Zululand, duly recognized and vested with a kind of authority that definitely does not emanate from the sources usually associated with liberalism, his proclamation might not have had the resonance and consequences that it did. Yes, there are liberals who are xenophobes. But there is no doubt that one could show that a xenophobic liberal must be a purveyor of some serious inconsistencies between her philosophical stand and her practical commitment to xenophobia. More importantly, we do not know that all the foreigners that the king said should leave South Africa were there illegally. Some were legitimate immigrants and could jolly well be on their way to naturalized citizenship. The exclusion of non-Zulu citizens from the ranks of those who could be legal occupiers of South African space would mean that citizenship is tied to blood and soil.

This takes us to the point that we made earlier respecting different grounds of residence and citizenship. To take a parallel example, Abdullahi Ahmed An-Na'im has argued that an Islamic state, by definition, cannot offer equal citizenship to all its residents. Under the system of *dhimma*, Muslims are the only true citizens and thus the only residents vested with full rights. Abbreviated citizenship is extended to other peoples of the Book—Jews and Christians—as long as they pay a poll tax, jizya, that Muslims are exempt from, and pledge allegiance to the state.[49] So, while chieftaincy held sway in Zululand, the king would have something to say about who could settle in his domain and under what conditions, and it is reasonable to assume that those conditions would have included allegiance to the king and his court.

But the modern liberal regime that dominates South Africa today is founded on the formal equality of all inhabitants, citizens or not, who bear rights that are the preserve of any human being and not qualified by contingencies like ethnicity, race, and gender, and whose status is not determined by their nationalities or other incidental circumstances. That is, in the modern setting, there are severe limits mandated by law and philosophy to what could be done even to illegal residents. Finally, citizens or not, residents of what used to be the Zulu king's domain owe zero allegiance to the king, beyond courtesy to him as their putative host if they are strangers and, therefore, could not be governed by a system that has been subsumed into a new system, with different legitimacy requirements.

The political philosophy of liberalism that undergirds the modern state does not allow the king to claim any superiority to other citizens, and the latter are not obliged to obey his directives, because they have had no say in his enthronement. And succession to his office is not open to all and sundry, limited only by their talents or lack thereof. It is why kings and queens in what are styled constitutional monarchies, dominated by liberalism, have had their political salience taken away; they have become mere figureheads in a dispensation under which they have nothing on those who inhabit their domains, including foreigners.

In the Lagos case, there are no constitutional provisions for chieftaincy in Nigeria. Rilwan Akiolu's imprecations against non-Lagosians in "his" realm might, then, even qualify as hate speech directed at those referenced in his address. The ground of his legitimacy as the ọba of Lagos is principally in the history and traditions of the city. But the city is now much more than its indigenes and their descendants and has been so for over five hundred years! More importantly, threatening people with untoward conse- quences up to and including death for refusing to vote for the king's favored candidate would violate one of the fundaments of constituting legitimate power in the modern state: the consent of the governed, freely expressed in fair electoral contests. What is more, he is ọba now at the pleasure of the state's governor. That is, the king claims supremacy that does not derive from proper liberal-democratic principles that we associate with representative government.

Can a Liberal be a Chief?
Can a Chief be a Liberal?

When we ask if a liberal can be a chief, and vice versa, what we seek to know is whether the undergirding philosophical principles of each are compatible with those of the other. Again, short of clinching this by definition, we need to ascertain what these principles are and how they may be instantiated.

We have seen that this is not a problem peculiar or limited to Africa. It is no less exigent in the Netherlands and Japan than it is in Nigeria. The critical difference is that neither Nigeria nor Ghana has a single chieftaincy, as do the Netherlands and Japan. This is a matter of great importance. It points, again, to the unwisdom of not minding the subtle but significant specificities of chieftaincy across the globe. Where a chieftaincy presides over a given territory, it is easy to capture and work out how it might relate to liberalism. In the early days of liberal republicanism in Europe, even though some of the states were organized in the manner of aristocracies or even monarchies, the freedom of the citizens to choose their rulers was gradually becoming a requirement, and the role of heredity had begun to recede into the background. By the same token, it was easy for the erstwhile subjects in such states to compel change and force their rulers to either hold on to their prerogatives and risk losing the realm entirely, or accede to demands to become figurehead rulers, relinquishing control to popularly elected councils and yet remaining relevant to the future of their respective polities. In various African polities, those options were not available, as a result of the shenanigans of colonial administrators.

We have, rather, diverse chieftaincies of differing salience in the political setup of their respective areas. Yet, since the eve of independence, various African countries have persisted in trying to establish liberal-democratic regimes. They have done so completely oblivious, except when the situations that triggered our inquiry occur, of the philosophical conundrums that we have focused on in this essay. Given that this is the case, the question of whether chieftaincy has any place in this new order is as urgent as ever. What is more, representatives of chieftaincies continue to clamor for constitutional roles in their respective countries.

What complicates the situation even more is that we have hardly any chieftaincies that continue to owe their legitimacy to their original, autochthonous constitutions. Rather, they have all been incorporated into modern state jurisdictions putatively built on liberal-democratic foundations. Their appointments must now be validated by the state, and even the boundaries of their domains and the limits of their power are now set by those states. In effect, they have become what Lugard intended for them as they were incorporated into the structures of indirect rule: dignified but subordinate advisers to state functionaries, be those elected or appointed. They can be destooled or dethroned at the pleasure of state authorities, and no matter how frequently their erstwhile subjects go to them for dispute resolution, unless they are additionally designated as Customary Court judges or Justices of the Peace, their pronouncements no longer have any authoritative cachet or the force of law. Such designations, where they occur, provide one of the justifications standardly offered for chieftaincies' continuing relevance. Unless one were to assume that there is something about the African situation that makes it peculiar, these are contingencies that the rest of the world routinely takes care of with many of the modern institutions sponsored or, at least, accommodated by liberal regimes—mediation, arbitration, alternative dispute resolution, and so on. In short, this is not enough to obviate the issues that we have identified in this section with the compatibility of chieftaincy and liberalism.

Given that African countries are increasingly opting for modes of governance based on liberal-democratic-representative principles, the question turns on whether chieftaincy, of the types that proliferate across Africa, has any place in such an order. We know that, even in those cases where some African scholars have argued that the chieftaincies are based

on the consent of the governed, most of the chieftaincies have their grounding principles in heredity,
primogeniture even, with severe gender colorations
and indigeneity requirements that restrict eligibility
for participation by the increasingly multiethnic,
multinational inhabitants of their realms.

If what we just said is true, it means that
the grounds of legitimacy on which chieftaincy
rests and chieftaincy's practical implications cannot
accommodate the requirements of a liberal-democratic republic. Even in the United Kingdom, where
chieftaincy continues to be an integral element of the
constitutional order, membership of the House of
Commons precludes any ascription-based hereditary
title holders from participating in its proceedings.

Might it help to make chieftaincy an elective
position?[50] It depends on the criteria for eligibility for
electors and for who could be elected. If all citizens
of a certain age and residence can contest for the
chieftaincy, then we enter a semantic debate, for then
there would be no difference between a chiefship and
any other elective office. But if many inhabitants are
prima facie excluded from having a voice in how the
chieftaincy is constituted or who is eligible to occupy
or exercise it, then the liberal requirement is elided.
For this wall between chieftaincy and liberalism to
be broken down, it would mean the deracination of
chieftaincy, just as modern citizenship has become
decoupled from blood and soil and is now solely tied
to signing up to the civil project of a society founded
on the equivalent of social contractarianism.

Might there be ways to ground legitimacy
outside elections; outside, that is, consent of the

governed? Might there be other ways to secure consent to rule, say by selection, as was often the case with chieftaincies in the past? I am arguing that the growing preference across the African continent for representative democracy framed by liberalism of one sort or another has made urgent again a reconsideration of the place of chieftaincy in the governance of African polities.

An ascription-based authority cannot sit well in the politics of a state based on liberal-democratic foundations. No, a chief *cannot* be a liberal; and a liberal *cannot* be a chief. I would like to give the final word to one who was a consummate liberal but had to juggle the requirements of and his preference for liberalism and the need to manage chieftaincy in governance in western Nigeria at independence.

> Besides, I had to reckon with the Ọbas and Chiefs who were very jealous of and extremely sensitive about their traditional rights and privileges. In spite of agitation here and there against this or that Ọba or Chief, the institution of Ọbaship and Chieftaincy was still held in high esteem by the people. But the traditional rights and privileges which the Ọbas and Chiefs wished to preserve were antithetic to democratic concepts and to the yearnings and aspirations of the people. To make a frontal attack on those rights and privileges would be the surest way of bringing a host of hornets' nests about our ears. To compromise with them, on the other hand, would mean death to our new party. The problem which faced me, therefore, was that whilst I must strive to harness the influence of the Ọbas and Chiefs for our purposes, I must, at the same time, take earliest possible steps to modify

their rights and abrogate such of their privileges as were considered repugnant, to an extent that would both satisfy the commonalty and make the Ọbas and Chiefs feel secure in their traditional offices.[51]

Starkly put, it is time to chuck chieftaincy as a political institution in the continent. ■

Endnotes

1. I am borrowing this term from J. Michael Williams, *Chieftaincy, the State, and Democracy: Political Legitimacy in Post-Apartheid South Africa* (Bloomington: Indiana University Press, 2010).
2. J. E. Casely Hayford, *Gold Coast Native Institutions* (1903; repr., London: Frank Cass, 1970), 63.
3. See, in general, Kofi A. Busia, *The Position of the Chief in the Modern Political System of Ashanti* (London: Oxford University Press for the International African Institute, 1951). Obviously, Busia was not impressed by Hayford's strictures regarding nomenclature, because he wrote throughout as if there were no issue with calling kings chiefs, even as he cited Hayford's work at least three times.
4. "It was quickly recognized by the seminar that it is very difficult to define a chief in the West African context: there is no apparent relationship between the role of the Emir of Kano and the Limba chiefs, both considered in this volume. It is only by accident that they have all been called 'chiefs,' a distinctly colonial 'diminutive' term, which effectively reduced the status of rulers like the Oba of Benin, who in pre colonial times considered himself, and was considered by his subjects, a king." Michael Crowder and Obaro Ikime, introduction to *West African Chiefs: Their Changing Status under Colonial Rule and Independence*, ed. Michael Crowder and Obaro Ikime (Ile-Ife: University of Ife Press, 1970), ix. There is a caution here that those of us in the theoretical disciplines need heed, before we quickly adopt terms and concepts without investigating their histories and their meanings through time.
5. The British separated their colonial possessions in Africa into two categories: "colonies" and "protectorates." Residents of colonies were putative British subjects, as citizens were then styled, and they enjoyed the full rights of citizenship as available in a modern polity. Protectorates were areas inhabited by natives who were adjudged too backward to be governed by modern rules and principles and were the quintessential candidates for what would later be called indirect rule. As we will see presently, this distinction sheds more light on the differential treatment of chieftaincy by colonizers and colonized respecting what to do with it in the dependencies.

6. See Lord Lugard, *The Dual Mandate in British Tropical Africa* (London: Frank Cass, 1922). Incidentally, anticipations of the idea that colonialism might be justified by some commitment to improving the conditions of the colonized can be found in the writings of many diasporic Africans in the nineteenth century who, subscribing to the idea of providential determinism, argued that slavery was God's inscrutable way to expose them to the light of Christianity, which in their consciousness was indistinguishable from modernity. They asked their fellows to exploit Africa's resources to preempt others from doing so, as part of their mission to restore Africa to the pride of place it enjoyed in history before the predations of the European slave trade forced the continent into catastrophic decline. And Alexander Crummell and others did so without the racist animus that motivated Lugard and his racist band of colonizers.

7. This is not a trivial distinction. I use "indigenous" to refer to those forms of rule that were in place in various polities before European colonialism was imposed, "autochthonous" when we have evidence that the forms were original to their locations. In essence, we may have indigenous practices that owe their inspiration to places and influences outside their borders and have modified what may have been autochthonous to those locations prior to that. For instance, the Sokoto Caliphate was indigenous but was not autochthonous; in that case, the autochthonous forms were the Hausa kingdoms that the new Fulani rulers colonized and imposed the caliphate system upon. These are some of the subtle but significant characteristics that epithets like "traditional" and "precolonial" elide.

8. Crowder and Ikime, introduction, vii–xxix.

9. Moses E. Ochonu, *Colonialism by Proxy: Hausa Imperial Agents and Middle Belt Consciousness in Nigeria* (Bloomington: Indiana University Press, 2014).

10. Olúfẹ́mi Táíwò, *How Colonialism Preempted Modernity in Africa* (Bloomington: Indiana University Press, 2010), chap. 6.

11. Some of Julius Nyerere's writings lend themselves to this interpretation. Kenneth Kaunda also leans in this direction. And Kofi Busia makes a case for this in his *Africa in Search of Democracy* (New York: Praeger, 1967), chap. 2. Edward Wamala actually talks of the Buganda system as a "monarchical democracy," in his "Government by Consensus: An Analysis of a Traditional

Form of Democracy," and Joe Teffo wants a place for chieftaincy in the South African constitutional order, in "Democracy, Kingship, and Consensus: A South African Perspective," both in *A Companion to African Philosophy*, ed. Kwasi Wiredu (Malden, MA: Blackwell, 2004), 435–42 and 443–49, respectively. See also Chris Okechukwu Uroh, "The Indigenous Igbo Political Philosophy and the Quest for Political Legitimacy," in *Indigenous Political Structures and Governance in Nigeria*, ed. Olufemi Vaughan (Ibadan: Bookcraft, 2004), 269–99.

12. Jean-Jacques Rousseau, *The Social Contract*, trans. G. D. H. Cole (London: Everyman, 1950), book 1, chap. 3, p. 168.

13. Joe Teffo, "Monarchy and Democracy: Towards a Cultural Renaissance," *Journal on African Philosophy* 1, no. 1 (2002): 4 (hereafter cited as *MD*).

14. Teffo, "Democracy, Kingship, and Consensus," 445–48. See also Moeketsi Letseka, "How Convincing Is the Claim That Coexistence between Traditional African Values and Liberal Democratic Values in South Africa Is a Contradiction?," *La Pensée* 76, no. 9 (2014): 382–95.

15. I am going to ignore for now other contentious issues raised by Teffo's discussion. For one thing, I do not think that liberal-democratic constitutions are varied just to accommodate segments of a population. So the insistence that chieftaincy be preserved and accommodated within a liberal constitution to accommodate the preferences of rural dwellers presupposes that rural dwellers are one of a kind, monolithic in their constitution, or that we can keep the question of equal protection from becoming salient if we allow stranger elements to settle in those rural domains. As the experience of South Africa, especially, shows, these are contingencies that have asserted themselves, and we see them in the opening two incidents that we have used to frame this discussion. For another treatment that questions the legitimacy of a liberal-democratic regime from the perspective of a segment of the population and its preferences for governance, see Jason Hickel, *Democracy as Death: The Moral Order of Anti-liberal Politics in South Africa* (Oakland: University of California Press, 2015). For another, the call for "contextual democracy" is a problematic one in the context of political philosophy, where it is generally required that theory always be universal and explain more than a single instance.

16. Williams, *Chieftaincy, the State, and Democracy*, 2 (hereafter cited as *CSD*).

17. See, on this, Kate Baldwin, *The Paradox of Traditional Chiefs in Democratic Africa* (New York: Cambridge University Press, 2016).

18. Adejare Oladosu, "Designing Viable Republican Constitutions for Modern African States: Why the Institution of Traditional Kingship Must Be Abolished," *African Journal of International Affairs* 8, nos. 1–2 (2005): 46 (hereafter cited as *DVRC*).

19. If Quentin Skinner is right, many republics at the dawn of the modern age were captained by monarchs. *Liberty before Liberalism* (Cambridge: Cambridge University Press, 1998).

20. For a discussion of the difference between acceptance of and acquiescence in a legal system, see H. L. A. Hart, *The Concept of Law* (Oxford: Oxford University Press, 1961); William Leon McBride, "The Acceptance of a Legal System," *The Monist* 49 (1965): 377–96.

21. I think it is unfortunate that, in his ardor to uproot "traditional kingship," Oladosu slipped into the standard racist fare respecting what Africans have not contributed to the march of civilization. Drawing a contrast between Europe and Africa regarding whether kingship should be given a pass for having spearheaded "the development of great civilisations," Oladosu made the following unfortunate remark, which, were it proffered by non-African scholars, would have us howling for their heads: "By contrast, not much has been recorded as the contribution of African kings and princes to the building of the material structures of civilization, or the development of its intellectual components. For the most part, it seems that the royals in African history have been content to just feed off the backs of their subjects. Many members of African royal houses merely savoured the best that the world had to offer, without adding a scintilla of value to it" (*DVRC*, 53).

22. Unfortunately, some contributions to the existing literature from political science and philosophy are dominated by an ahistorical approach to their subject matter, and this limits the illumination they can yield for our understanding of the problem under review. John A. A. Ayoade and Adigun A. B. Agbaje, eds., *African Traditional Political Thought and Institutions* (Lagos: Centre for Black and African Arts and Civilization, 1989), and Busia, *Position of the Chief*, are two good examples.

23. Can we really escape essentialism? Even if we limit ourselves to working definitions, we still must circumscribe the boundaries of the terms we deploy in our conceptual elucidations, and this cannot be done without isolating some essential qualities of our terms and concepts. But that is not an issue for discussion here.

24. In the African discourse, Ghanaian commentators are fond of pointing out that chiefs are elected in their jurisdiction. Let us for the moment ignore the fact that most of their examples come from the Akan sector of the country, leaving almost two-thirds of the country with their respective chiefly traditions unaccounted for. Either they choose to ignore, or are unaware of the limits imposed by, the fact that only a few families can put forward candidates for enstoolment—they cite this and just proceed to talk as if it does not matter—a factor that emphasizes our point about the centrality of heredity. Nor is it the case that all members of the constituency are eligible voters, if voters at all. Again, this is not an absolute disqualifier of such an arrangement being compatible with liberalism. Lastly, the positions are not open to all.

25. Oladosu's prioritizing of popular sovereignty as the core marker of liberalism is inadequate, for reasons that Skinner lays out in *Liberty before Liberalism*. Oladosu is right in his contention that republicanism-as-popular-sovereignty was a later development, but he will agree with me that when the founders of liberalism made consent the basis of legitimacy, popular sovereignty was the furthest thing from their minds (Oladosu, personal communication).

26. Busia, *Position of the Chief*, 128 (my emphasis). So are Ashanti who live away from their chiefs, in other domains dominated by other national groups, which introduces more complications. I am sure there are other variations, in other parts of the continent, yet another reminder of the folly of blind generalizations.

27. See Ochonu, *Colonialism by Proxy*; A. E. Afigbo, *The Warrant Chiefs* (London: Longman, 1972); Crowder and Ikime, *West African Chiefs*.

28. For a fuller discussion, See Táíwò, *How Colonialism Preempted Modernity in Africa*, chaps. 2 and 3.

29. See, generally, A. I. Asiwaju, *West African Transformations: Comparative Impacts of French and British Colonialism* (Lagos: Malthouse Press, 2001); James Africanus Beale Horton,

Letters on the Political Condition of the Gold Coast (1870; repr., London: Frank Cass, 1970); Casely Hayford, *Gold Coast Native Institutions.*

30. See, e.g., D. T. Niane, *Sundiata: An Epic of Old Mali*, trans. G. D. Pickett (Essex: Longman, 1994), 90n32: "M. Niane uses throughout the Mandingo name for Alexander, 'Djoulou Kara Naini,' which is a corruption of the Arabic 'Dhu'l Qarnein'" (Pickett); "In all the Mandingo traditions they like to compare Sundiata to Alexander. It is said that Alexander was the second last great conqueror of the world and Sundiata the seventh and last" (Niane).

31. Jacob Egharevba, *A Short History of Benin* (Ibadan: Ibadan University Press, 1968). In his I*n Search of Ogun: Soyinka in Spite of Nietzsche* (Lagos: Hornbill House, 2014), Odia Ofeimun has moved from Soyinka's appropriation of Ogun to asking us to research it as history. He argues that this history holds significant implications not only for our understanding of the history of Benin and its relations with other polities long before colonialism came upon the kingdom but also for our analysis of the grounds of legitimacy in a celebrated indigenous political formation. This he does by characterizing the rule of Ewuare as a period of epochal transformation in the evolution of Benin in the fifteenth century. I hope to return to this account and analysis in a future work.

32. I. A. Akinjogbin, *Dahomey and Its Neighbours, 1708–1878* (Cambridge: Cambridge Press, 1967); Karl Polanyi, *Dahomey and the Slave Trade: An Analysis of an Archaic Economy* (Seattle: University of Washington Press, 1966).

33. Asiwaju, *West African Transformations*, 19.

34. Asiwaju, *West African Transformations*, 20.

35. Lamin Sanneh, *Abolitionists Abroad: Blacks and the Making of Modern West Africa* (Cambridge, MA: Harvard University Press, 1999).

36. It is quite easy to misunderstand their ideas and their standpoint. If one does not deracialize the idea of modernity, it is easy to assimilate their positions to those of their racist interlocutors of the period. My argument is that these men, having embraced modernity and its tenets, strived, unlike their racist traducers, to move Africa forward to a more salubrious future along modern lines. Alexander Crummell, Edward Wilmot

Blyden, James Africanus Beale Horton, and Martin R. Delany all fall within this category. But even those who fell outside it, the likes of Casely Hayford or John Mensah Sarbah, all embraced new modes of social living and principles of social ordering legitimated by modernity and its core tenets.

37. Táíwò, *How Colonialism Preempted Modernity in Africa*, 11.

38. For a discussion of the society in Ibadan politics, see O. A. Adeboye, "'Elders-Still-Exist': Socio-cultural Groups and Political Participation in Colonial Ibadan," in Vaughan, *Indigenous Political Structures and Governance in Nigeria*, 195–230. Commentators often miss the ambiguity of the term "àgbà" by simply translating it as "elder." Yes, it does mean that, and, in the context of a Yorùbá culture that confers more salience on age-defined hierarchy than any other, it is easy to see why many would leave the issue there. But, as in other natural languages, few words in Yorùbá escape the ambiguities and ambivalences that afflict the meanings of words in its lexicon. "Àgbà" also designates "expert," "learned," "hugely successful," "accomplished," and "knowledgeable." A perusal of the aims and objectives of the society, including a tantalizing commitment to science as a tool for social progress, would show that "àgbà" did not solely reference age, tradition, or wisdom in the old ways of doing things.

39. See Ọbafẹmi Awolowo, *AWO: The Autobiography of Chief Ọbafẹmi Awolowo* (Cambridge: Cambridge University Press, 1960).

40. See, especially, the collection *Africa Speaks*, ed. James Duffy and Robert A. Manners (Princeton, NJ: D. Van Nostrand, 1961).

41. Olufemi Vaughan, "Chieftaincy Politics in Nigeria," in Vaughan, *Indigenous Political Structures and Governance in Nigeria*, 47–73.

42. See Afigbo, *Warrant Chiefs*; Mahmood Mamdani, *Citizen and Subject* (Princeton, NJ: Princeton University Press, 1996); Crowder and Ikime, introduction.

43. Asiwaju, *West African Transformations*, 36.

44. Asiwaju, *West African Transformations*, 36–37.

45. Lord Lugard, *Political Memoranda: Revision of Instructions to Political Officers on Subjects Chiefly Political and Administrative, 1913–1918* (London: Frank Cass, 1970), 296 (hereafter cited as *PM*).

46. "Whilst it is impossible to define 'chief' in pre-colonial terms, it is possible to define it in colonial terms for the purposes of this symposium. Chief, under both French and British colonial rule, was used administratively to designate African administrative authorities recognized by the colonial governments." Crowder and Ikime, introduction, x.

47. For appreciations of this phenomenon that contrast with what I have presented here, see Ezekiel Mkhwanazi, "Nkrumah and the Chiefs: Contending Epistemologies of Democracy," *Journal on African Philosophy*, no. 4 (2012): 18–28; Louis J. Munoz, "Traditional Participation in a Modern Political System—the Case of Western Nigeria," *Journal of Modern African Studies* 18, no. 3 (1980): 443–68; Letseka, "How Convincing Is the Claim."

48. Contrast this with the Indian case. "When the British left in 1947, all native states signed treaties of accession to the newly independent nations of India or Pakistan, sometimes under the threat of military action. By 1950, all the native states within the borders of India had been integrated into independent India, and were subject to the same administrative, legal, and political systems as those of the erstwhile British Indian areas. The rulers of these states were no longer sovereign rulers, but many of them continued to play an active role in the politics of post-Independence India. They were granted annual incomes ("privy purses") by the Indian government as partial compensation for their loss of state revenue, but this privilege, along with all other princely honors, was discontinued in 1971." Lakshmi Iyer, "Direct versus Indirect Colonial Rule in India: Long-term Consequences," Working Paper 05-041, Harvard Business School (2008): 9–10.

49. Abdullahi Ahmed An-Na'im, *Islam and the Secular: State Negotiating the Future of Shari'a* (Cambridge, MA: Harvard University Press, 2008), chap. 3.

50. See, for a discussion of the South African experience in this connection, Williams, *Chieftaincy, the State, and Democracy.*

51. Awolowo, *AWO*, 261–62.

Also available from Prickly Paradigm Press:

continued

continued